INQUIRY: WESTERN CIVILIZATION

Democracy and Nationalism

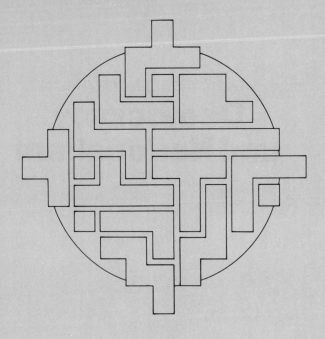

Other titles in the
INQUIRY: Western Civilization Series

THE EMERGING YEARS
THE GROWTH OF INDUSTRIALIZATION
IMPERIALISM AND THE EMERGING NATIONS
THE RISE OF TOTALITARIAN STATES
WAR AND PEACE IN THE 20TH CENTURY

Sidney Schwartz • John R. O'Connor

INQUIRY: WESTERN CIVILIZATION
Democracy and Nationalism

GLOBE BOOK COMPANY, INC.

NEW YORK / CHICAGO / CLEVELAND

ABOUT THE AUTHORS

SIDNEY SCHWARTZ has served as a social studies teacher, guidance counselor, and department chairman of social studies and other academic subjects. He has written social studies texts including Globe's *Exploring Our Nation's History,* and is the author of several workbooks and teachers' manuals. For many years he has been active as a member of the Association of Chairmen in the New York City Schools.

JOHN R. O'CONNOR is a principal in the New York City school system. He is widely known for his lectures and for a number of excellent textbooks he has edited, including *Exploring American History, Exploring a Changing World,* and *Exploring the Non-Western World.* He is also coauthor of *Exploring World History* and *Exploring the Urban World.*

Editors: Elizabeth J. Lott and Laurence Alan Werner
Photo editor: Adelaide Garvin Ungerland
Maps: Dyno Lowenstein, Pictograph Corp.
Illustrations: Ned Glattauer
Cover: Arthur Ritter

ISBN: 0-87065-562-0

Copyright © 1976, Globe Book Company, Inc.
50 West 23rd Street, New York, N.Y. 10010

Published simultaneously in Canada

Printed in the United States of America   3 4 5 6 7 8 9 0

Contents

Looking Ahead

The development of science and technology is one of the outstanding achievements of Western civilization. This breakthrough in knowledge has resulted in changes that have transformed the world during the past two hundred years. It will probably produce even greater advances in the future. Among its effects are far-reaching changes in society and government. One very important change has been the rise of the common people to a position of importance and power.

Until the eighteenth century, the common people played only a limited role in history. Their labor supported society, yet they had little influence. Governments were run by the upper classes, and writers were generally more interested in these powerful groups than in lesser ones. The Industrial Revolution brought great changes, for it created two new classes of society. These are the small, wealthy capitalist class of factory owners and the very large class of factory workers. The factory owners greatly strengthened the middle class. It became strong enough to challenge the power of the nobility and clergy. The workers were crowded together in cities and suffering from bad treatment. They formed unions and other organizations, and soon demanded a voice in the government.

This book shows how the lower classes brought about two important political movements, democracy and nationalism. Like the Industrial Revolution, these new movements arose in Western Europe and spread to the rest of the world.

In discussing these movements the following are explored:

1. How did democracy develop in Great Britain (England)?

2. How did France achieve democracy?

3. How did Italy and Germany become united nations in the late nineteenth century?

4. Why did the Austrian and Turkish empires break up?

5. How are democracy and nationalism still changing the world today?

A British prime minister speaking to the House of Commons. In what ways is discussion important to a democracy?

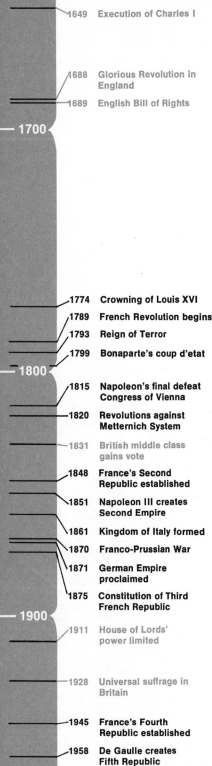

1649   Execution of Charles I

1688   Glorious Revolution in England

1689   English Bill of Rights

1700

1774   Crowning of Louis XVI

1789   French Revolution begins

1793   Reign of Terror

1799   Bonaparte's coup d'etat

1800

1815   Napoleon's final defeat Congress of Vienna

1820   Revolutions against Metternich System

1831   British middle class gains vote

1848   France's Second Republic established

1851   Napoleon III creates Second Empire

1861   Kingdom of Italy formed

1870   Franco-Prussian War

1871   German Empire proclaimed

1875   Constitution of Third French Republic

1900

1911   House of Lords' power limited

1928   Universal suffrage in Britain

1945   France's Fourth Republic established

1958   De Gaulle creates Fifth Republic

CHAPTER **1**

How Did Democracy Evolve in Great Britain?

DEMOCRACY means the "rule of the people." The word comes from ancient Greece, where the first democratic governments arose. The citizens of the Greek city of Athens met regularly to decide what policies the city should follow. The citizens chose the highest officials. They also sat on the juries that decided whether accused people were innocent or guilty. This kind of government is known as DIRECT DEMOCRACY because the people run the government themselves. It can still be found today in some American towns where the citizens run the local government by holding town meetings.

Direct democracy is generally most successful in small societies. Most democracies today have a great many people. They cannot easily meet every time a decision has to be made about government matters. Therefore, the modern form is usually that of REPRESENTATIVE DEMOCRACY. The people elect a few of their members to represent them in a LEGISLATURE. This body makes the laws for the whole society. Either the people or the legislature choose the EXECUTIVE. This is the

2

person or group that enforces the law and directs the government. In some democracies, the people also elect judges and sit on juries. The branch of government that administers justice is known as the JUDICIARY.

Modern democracy also has the three following features:

1. *Majority rule.* Decisions are made by voting. The group that wins a MAJORITY (more than half) of the votes wins the decision.

2. *Liberty.* A truly democratic government protects the rights of its people, especially their freedom of speech and press. This means that a MINORITY (a group with less than half the votes) is allowed to express its views. Every new idea has the support of a minority at first. If the idea is a good one, the minority can in time win over more and more people to its viewpoint. If the minority grows to become the majority, the new ideas can be put into effect. In this way, democracy encourages change and progress.

3. *Equality.* In a modern democracy, all citizens—regardless of their social class, religion, race, nationality, or sex—have equal rights.

To develop governments with all these features took hundreds of years. In fact, the democracies that exist today are still growing and changing. This chapter shows you how democracy developed through the centuries in England, or Great Britain, as that country is often called today.

The British Parliament building. What is the role of a legislature such as the British Parliament in a modern democracy?

1. WHAT WAS THE IMPORTANCE OF MAGNA CARTA?

It is a strange fact that England made its first great move toward democracy under one of its worst rulers. King John made the barons (lords) very angry. In 1215, they rose against him. After defeating his forces in battle, they forced him to sign MAGNA CARTA (a Latin term meaning "the great charter"). Magna Carta is a list of the rights of the barons and other freemen (people who were not serfs or slaves). The king promised not to violate these rights. From that time onward. English kings—no matter how powerful some of them became—had certain basic restraints.

Read the following selections from Magna Carta. Then decide whether the English are right in considering it the most important step in the development of their democracy.

King John signing the Magna Carta. How do you think he felt about signing the document?

We have granted to all freemen of our kingdom, for us and for our heirs forever, all the liberties written below.

No special feudal taxes shall be imposed in our kingdom except by the common council of the kingdom.

No official of ours shall take grain or other property from anyone without immediate payment.

No freeman shall be unjustly arrested, or imprisoned, or have his land taken, or be outlawed, banished [put out of the country], or in any way ruined. The lawful judgment of his peers [equals] shall be first required. Any action taken must be in agreement with the law of the land.

To no one will we sell, deny, or delay right or justice.

We ask if anyone has been removed by us, without legal judgment of his peers, from his lands, castles, or rights. We will restore these things to such persons immediately.

Adapted from Boyd C. Barrington, *The Magna Charta*, Philadelphia, 1900.

▶ **THINKING IT THROUGH**

1. Judging from Magna Carta, what did King John do that made the barons angry?
2. Which provision of Magna Carta led to the rise of Parliament (England's legislature)? To trial by jury? Refer directly to Magna Carta to support each answer.
3. Magna Carta was the first step toward democracy in England. Does this make it especially important? Why or why not?

2. *HOW WAS PARLIAMENT FORMED?*

England's legislature is called PARLIAMENT (from the French word *parler*, meaning "to talk"). In its early years, Parliament was a meeting of important Englishmen to discuss their country's problems. They also gave the king their advice. After Magna Carta, they voted on any new taxes the king wanted.

At first, Parliament consisted of "the lords spiritual and temporal"—that is, of high Church officials and nobles. These later met as a single body called the HOUSE OF LORDS. Eventually, the middle class grew wealthier and larger. The king began to include its representatives in the meetings. They became the present HOUSE OF COMMONS. (Until the twentieth century, the Lords was far more powerful than the Commons.)

The Parliament of 1295 is known as the "Model Parliament." This is because it included representatives of all three classes. The following is the notice King Edward I sent to the sheriffs (his local officials) to summon the members of the Model Parliament.

We intend to meet with the earls, barons, and other principal men of our kingdom. We will discuss with them ways to meet the dangers that are in these days threatening the kingdom. We strictly require you to have two knights from your county, two citizens from each city in the county, and two burgesses [freemen] from each borough elected [chosen] without delay. Be certain they are men who are especially trustworthy and capable of hard work. Have them come to us at the proper time and place.

Adapted from James Harvey Robinson (ed.), *Readings in European History.*

The Parliament of Edward I. In what ways do you think the common people gained by having representatives in government?

▶ **THINKING IT THROUGH**

1. Name the two houses of Parliament. Explain the reason for each name.
2. What groups were summoned by the king in 1295? Which was probably the most important group at that time? Why?
3. In his decree, the king said he wanted commoners who were "trustworthy and capable of hard work."
   a. Why did he make this requirement of the commoners?
   b. Why didn't he set the same requirement for the upper classes?

3. WHY WAS CHARLES I CONDEMNED TO DEATH?

During the seventeenth century, Louis XIV of France and other kings were gaining absolute power. The English kings also tried to strengthen their authority. But Parliament opposed them. To keep the kings from becoming too strong, Parliament made special use of its "power of the purse." (This is the power to approve or refuse new taxes.)

The struggle between the English kings and Parliament lasted almost a hundred years. An important conflict took place in the 1640's. King Charles I entered Parliament to arrest the leaders who opposed him. They fled and civil war broke out between the king's supporters and those of Parliament. The defenders of Parliament won. They brought the king to trial for treason. They found him guilty and beheaded him. The next selection is taken from the record of the king's trial, which was held in the House of Commons. Which side do you think had the better argument?

January 20, 1649

President of the House of Commons: Clerk, read the charge against the prisoner.
Clerk: Charles Stuart, King of England, you are charged as guilty

of all the blood that has been shed. You are guilty of having taken up arms against Parliament. . . .

King: (smiling as the charge is read) By what lawful authority have I been brought here?

President: In the name of the Commons of England.

King: I see no lords here that would make a Parliament. I am not convinced that you are a lawful authority.

(The king is asked several times to answer the charge, but refuses to do so. The president dismisses the court.)

January 22, 1649

President: Sir, I again ask you to answer the charge made against you by the Commons of England.

King: A king cannot be tried by any superior court on earth. It is not my case alone that I stand for, but the freedom of all the people of England. Power without law cannot make or change the law. If it does, no subject can be safe for his life or for anything that he calls his own. (The king is removed from the court.)

January 23, 1649

Solicitor General [the government's lawyer]: The prisoner does not answer the charges against him. Instead, he still disputes the authority of the court. According to law, if the prisoner does not plead guilty or not guilty, speedy judgment shall be pronounced against him.

Charles I receiving a religious blessing before he is killed. How do you think the witnesses felt about executing the king?

President: Sir, in plain terms, you are to give your true and final answer. Are you guilty or not guilty of these treasons that you are charged with?

King: (after a brief pause) When I was here yesterday, I tried to speak for the liberties of the people of England. I was interrupted. I want to know whether I may speak freely or not.

President: Sir, you have had the answer of this court. Answer your charge.

King: For the charge, I value it not a straw. It is the liberty of the people of England that I stand for. I cannot acknowledge a new court that I never heard of before. I am your king. I should be an example to all the people of England to uphold justice and to keep the laws. Therefore, until I know that this court is not against the basic laws of the kingdom, I can give no answer.

President: This is the third time you have denied this court. However, your actions have shown how well you have kept the liberties of the people. Truly, sir, men's intentions ought to be known by their actions. You have written your meaning in blood throughout the kingdom!

(The president adjourns the court.)

January 27, 1649

The president makes a long speech on the king's misrule. He says that kings must account to their people and to the law. He gives several instances of kings who have been deposed and imprisoned by their subjects, especially in Scotland.

The clerk reads the sentence. It includes the charge and the crimes of which the king had been found guilty.

The court decides that he, Charles Stuart, is a tyrant, traitor, murderer, and public enemy. He is to be put to death by severing his head from his body.

Adapted from B. Whitelock, *Memorials of the English Affairs* 1682.

▶ THINKING IT THROUGH

1. King Charles I refused to recognize the House of Commons as a court.
   a. What reasons does he give for refusing to do so?
   b. Do you think it was wise for the king to do this? Explain.
2. Do you think the House of Commons acted properly in continuing the trial and sentencing the king to death? Explain.
3. Which side do you think had the stronger argument, the king or Parliament? Why?
4. What effect do you think the execution of Charles I had on the development of democracy in England? Explain.

Oliver Cromwell (front left) dismissing Parliament to rule England as a dictator. Do you think he should have done so? Why or why not?

4. WHY WAS THE BILL OF RIGHTS IMPORTANT?

With the execution of Charles I, England became a REPUBLIC (a country without a king). The head of the new government was a military leader named Oliver Cromwell. He soon set aside parliamentary government and began to rule as a dictator. The English people did not like this. They had gone through the revolution to increase the power of Parliament, not to exchange their monarch for a military dictator. After Cromwell's death, they restored the son of Charles I to the throne. He was crowned as Charles II. This king was careful not to offend Parliament. However, his successor, James II, tried to reduce the power of Parliament. Though England was a Protestant country, James openly practiced the Catholic religion. He also appointed Catholics to high positions in the government.

Parliament and the people were angry. They tolerated the king's actions for a time. They thought he would be succeeded by his daughter Mary, who was a Protestant. Instead, James' second wife bore him a son, who was baptized a Catholic.

Parliament then forced James to flee from the country, and called to the throne Mary and her husband, William of Orange. This peaceful change is known as the GLORIOUS REVOLUTION of 1688. Before the new king and queen were allowed to ascend the throne, Parliament made them agree to a very important law, the BILL OF RIGHTS. Its main provisions follow.

The Lords spiritual and temporal and the Commons, are now gathered in a full and free representation of the nation. They hereby assert their ancient rights and liberties, and declare:

That suspending the laws or their execution by royal authority, without the consent of Parliament, is illegal.

That levying money for use by the crown, without grant of Parliament, is illegal.

That it is the right of the subjects to petition the king. All punishment for such petitioning is illegal.

That raising or keeping a standing army within the kingdom, in time of peace, unless it be with the consent of Parliament, is against the law.

That elections of members of Parliament ought to be free of any interference by the king.

That the freedom of speech and of debate in Parliament ought not to be questioned in any court or place outside of Parliament.

That excessive [very high] bail should not be required. [Bail allows a person accused of a crime to stay out of jail until his trial.] Excessive fines should not be imposed. Cruel and unusual punishments should not be inflicted.

It is against the safety and welfare of this Protestant kingdom to be governed by a popish [Catholic] ruler, or by any king or queen marrying a Catholic. Therefore, any person who professes the popish religion or who marries a Catholic shall be forever forbidden to inherit, possess, or enjoy the crown and government of this realm.

Whoever shall possess this crown shall join the Church of England, as established by law.

Adapted from D. C. Munro (ed.), *Translations and Reprints from the Original Sources of European History*, 1897.

William III and Mary II receiving the crown of England from members of Parliament. How do you think the king and queen felt about signing a Bill of Rights before they were crowned?

▶THINKING IT THROUGH

1. The Glorious Revolution was part of a struggle between Parliament and the crown.
    a. How did the revolution show that Parliament had become stronger than the king?
    b. Why was this event an important step forward in the development of British democracy?
2. The Bill of Rights was passed by Parliament to limit the power of the monarchy.
    a. What actions of the Stuart kings did Parliament want to prevent?
    b. Which provision of the bill do you consider the most important? Why?
    c. Are there any parts of the Bill of Rights that you feel are *not* democratic? Explain.

5. WHO HEADS THE BRITISH GOVERNMENT?

The Glorious Revolution of 1688 made it clear that England had become a LIMITED MONARCHY. This means it had a hereditary ruler, but the ruler's powers were restricted. What powers does the British monarch still have today? Who is the real head of the British government? These questions are discussed in the selections that follow.

a. The Position of the Monarch

It might be difficult for an American to understand the position which the English monarch holds today. The British tend to cling to old customs, while changing the way the system actually works. For example, Queen Elizabeth II is still an absolute monarch in theory. So she must sign every bill before it can become law. But, in practice, no monarch has refused to sign a bill since the year 1707! After reading the selections that follow, try to decide how powerful the British ruler actually is.

The occupant of the throne accepts and acts on the advice of his ministers. He is entitled to give his ministers all information that comes to him. He can point out objections against the course which they advise. He can also suggest (if he thinks fit) another policy. Such suggestions are always received by

Queen Elizabeth II. What is the role of the British monarch today?

ministers with the utmost respect. But, in the end, the sovereign [ruler] always acts upon the advice which the ministers feel it their duty to offer.

The personal duties of the sovereign in the actual administration of the government are now limited mainly to putting his signature on various documents. The true importance of the sovereign is to be found in his position as the representative of the nation's power and dignity, independent of and above the changes of party government.

Adapted from *The United Kingdom Constitution: Some Selected Quotations.* By permission of the British Information Services.

b. The Position of the Prime Minister and Cabinet

When the monarch's powers were limited, the PRIME MINISTER *became the real chief executive. He became responsible for carrying out the laws. Today the prime minister and his cabinet are members of the House of Commons. The prime minister is the head of the political party which has a majority of the seats in the House of Commons. Therefore, he and his cabinet also control the making of laws. How powerful is the prime minister? The next selection helps answer this question.*

In the cabinet and out of it, the most important person is the prime minister. It is he who is mainly concerned with forming a cabinet and with the subjects which the cabinet discusses. The relations between the queen and the cabinet, and between the cabinet and Parliament, are also mainly his concern.

The most marked feature of the modern British system of government is the control of both the executive and legislative functions by a small body of men, the members of the cabinet. They secretly decide the most important questions of policy. The most important check on their power is the existence of a powerful and organized opposition in Parliament.

There is always the possibility that measures proposed by the government may meet with the people's disapproval. This may enable the opposition [party] to defeat them at the next general election, and to replace them in their control of the executive.

Adapted from *The United Kingdom Constitution: Some Selected Quotations.* By permission of the British Information Services.

Prime Minister Harold Wilson, whose Labour Party was returned to power in 1974, when it defeated the Conservatives at the polls. What is the role of the British prime minister?

▶ THINKING IT THROUGH

1. The British ruler *always* acts on the advice of his ministers.
   a. Why does he do so?
   b. It has been said that the king would sign his own death warrant if the prime minister put it before him. Do you think this is so? Why or why not?
2. "The British monarch reigns but does not rule."
   a. Explain this statement.
   b. Do you think the British monarch is only a figurehead? Explain.
3. Compare the power of the British prime minister with that of the President of the United States, by answering the following questions:
   a. In what way is the prime minister more powerful than the President?
   b. Why is the prime minister not free to do whatever he wants?

6. HOW IS THE PRIME MINISTER CHOSEN?

The British government is based on a two-party system. This means that it has only two main political parties. In the nineteenth century, these were the CONSERVATIVES (Tories) and the LIBERALS (Whigs). The Conservatives represented mainly the upper classes and were slow in making changes. The Liberals were backed mainly by the middle class and usually favored reforms. Early in the twentieth century, the trade unions formed the LABOUR PARTY to promote the interests of the workers. Labour made rapid gains. It soon replaced the Liberals as the second main party.

Today the prime minister is the leader of either the Conservatives or the Labourites, depending on which party wins a majority of the seats in Commons. He holds office as long as he keeps his majority. How this works in practice is shown in the next passage, which is about the election of 1970. The Labour leader, Harold Wilson, had been prime minister for six years. His party had already won two elections. He called for a third election in 1970 because he expected his party to win again. The passage tells you what happened and why.

HEATH WINS UPSET ELECTION VICTORY

LONDON, June 19, 1970. Edward Heath officially took over the British government as the new prime minister after his Conservative Party was returned to power. The sensational upset victory over the Labour Party gave the Conservatives their proudest moments since World War II. Heath immediately went to his official residence at 10 Downing Street for conferences on the formation of a new government. He is expected to announce his cabinet appointments in a few days.

With all districts reporting, the Conservatives held an overall working majority in the House of Commons of 30 seats. Final standings gave the Conservatives 330 seats, Labour 288, Liberals 6, and others 6.

After forming a government, the prime minister will soon have to turn his attention to a number of economic issues. It is quite possible that economic worries in the nation are largely responsible for the Conservatives' stunning victory. Throughout the campaign, Heath warned the country of grave economic troubles resulting from the policies of the Labour Party. Among these are rising prices, heavy taxation, and disorder in labor relations.

Adapted from an article by Richard Reston in the *Los Angeles Times*, June 21, 1970. Copyright 1970, *Los Angeles Times*. Reprinted by permission.

▶**THINKING IT THROUGH**

1. The prime minister and cabinet changed after the election of June 1970.
   a. Why did this happen?
   b. Did this change express the wishes of the British people? Why or why not?
2. Is it a good idea to change the government in this way, so that the prime minister always controls a majority of the House of Commons? Explain.
3. The British government described above is a two-party system.
   a. What is a two-party system?
   b. Does the United States have such a system? Give facts to support your answer.
   c. Is it better to have only two major parties or to have a larger number of parties representing groups that have different views? Explain.

7. HOW DID THE MIDDLE CLASS WIN THE RIGHT TO VOTE?

Great Britain was a limited monarchy in the eighteenth century. Still it was not a democracy by modern standards. For example, only a small part of the population could vote and hold office. This consisted of well-to-do property owners who belonged to the Church of England.

A struggle to reform the voting system began early in the nineteenth century. Reformers made speeches, wrote articles and books, and led parades and demonstrations. Finally, in 1831, they gained enough votes to enable the Whig Party to win the election. The new Whig prime minister introduced a bill to reform the voting system and allow middle-class men to vote.

The next selection is a letter by a Whig member of Commons to a friend. In it he describes what happened when the Reform Bill came to a vote. The vote was so close that there was a "division." This means that the supporters of the bill remained in Commons to be counted while the opponents went out into the lobby to be counted there. Which side would you expect to win?

Members of the Whig Party cheering at the news that the House of Commons has just passed the first Reform Bill. For what reasons is majority rule important in a democracy?

Dear Ellis,

Such a scene as the division of last Tuesday I never saw and never expect to see again. The crowd overflowed the House in every part. When the strangers were cleared out and the door locked, we had 608 members present. This was 55 more than there ever were in a division before. The opposition went out into the lobby. We [the supporters of the Reform Bill] spread ourselves over the benches on both sides of the House. Many of us had not been able to find a seat during the evening.

When the doors were shut, we began to try to figure out how many supporters we had. Everyone said, "We have lost it. We are only 280 at most." "I do not think we are 250. They are 300." This was the talk on our benches. The tellers [the clerks who counted the votes] passed along our last row. The suspense was hard to bear; the vote was now 291–292. We were all standing up and stretching forward, counting with the tellers. At 300 there was a short cry of joy. At 302 another cry of joy went up. This was cut short in a moment, however, for we did not yet know what the opposite vote might be. We did know that we could not be badly beaten.

The doors were thrown open and they [the opposition] came in. Each of them, as he entered, brought some different report of their numbers. First we heard that they were 303. Then that number rose to 310, then went down to 307. We were all breathless with anxiety. You might have heard a pin drop as the head teller read the final count of 302–301.

Shouts broke out and many of us shed tears. We shook hands and clapped each other on the back. We went out laughing, crying, and cheering into the lobby. All the passages and stairs into the waiting rooms were packed with people. They had waited until four in the morning to know the result. We passed through a narrow lane between the two thick masses of them. All the way down they were shouting and waving their hats, till we got into the open air. I called a cab. The first thing the driver asked was, "Is the bill carried?" "Yes, by one vote." "Thank God for it, sir!" he said.

Adapted and abridged from E. P. Cheyney, *Readings in English History*, pp. 688–700.

▶ THINKING IT THROUGH

1. Why was the passing of the Reform Bill by the House of Commons a very exciting occasion?
2. Why were the British people extremely disappointed when the House of Lords later voted down the bill?
3. What would you expect the people to do about this defeat? Why?

8. *HOW DID THE BRITISH GAIN UNIVERSAL SUFFRAGE?*

When the House of Lords refused to pass the Reform Bill, protest meetings were held all over the country. Many businessmen refused to pay taxes. There were even a few riots. At the prime minister's request, the king threatened to appoint hundreds of Whigs to the House of Lords to vote for the bill. This threat forced the Lords to pass the bill. Similar struggles led to the passing of four more reform bills during the next hundred years. There were reform bills passed in 1857, 1884, and 1918. In each of these, additional groups in British society were permitted to vote. Finally, with the bill of 1928, Great Britain achieved UNIVERSAL SUFFRAGE—the right of all citizens aged 21 and over to vote.

The graph on page 16 shows the effects of each reform bill. Which bill looks to you like the most important one?

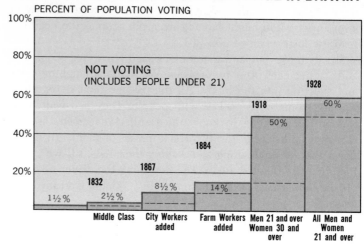

STEPS TOWARD UNIVERSAL SUFFRAGE IN BRITAIN

PERCENT OF POPULATION VOTING

NOT VOTING
(INCLUDES PEOPLE UNDER 21)

1928

1918

1884

1867

1832

1½%   2½%   8½%   14%   50%   60%

Middle Class | City Workers added | Farm Workers added | Men 21 and over Women 30 and over | All Men and Women 21 and over

▶ INTERPRETING THE GRAPH

1. Before 1832, what percentage of the British people had the right to vote?
2. Which reform bill resulted in the smallest increase in the percentage of voters? Which brought about the largest increase? Give the percent of change in each case.
3. The law of 1832 is often considered the most important one. Do you think it is? Why or why not?
4. When were city workers granted the vote? When were women?
5. It took five laws, passed over a period of a hundred years, for the British people to gain universal suffrage. What are the advantages and disadvantages of improving democracy very slowly?
6. A recent law in the United States lowered the voting age in presidential elections from 21 to 18. Do you approve of this development? Why or why not?

9. HOW DID WOMEN FIGHT FOR EQUAL RIGHTS?

The most difficult struggle for equal rights in England was that of the SUFFRAGETTES (women who wanted the right to vote). The suffragettes began their fight in the middle of the nineteenth century. At that time, the legal status of women was similar to that of children. When a woman married, her property went to her husband. In case of a divorce, he usually kept both the property and the children. If he died, his widow needed another male to serve as her legal guardian.

The suffragettes began their struggle for equal rights by using peaceful methods. But they failed to win any reforms. In the early 1900's, they turned to more militant (fighting) methods.

The following passage was written by a leading suffragette, Mrs. Emmeline Pankhurst. She describes one of the methods women used to attract public attention to their demands. What do you think of their methods?

Late in the afternoon of Friday, March 1, I drove in a taxicab, accompanied by two other women. We went to the official home of the prime minister. It was exactly half past five when we got out of the cab. We threw our stones, four of them, through the window panes. As we expected, we were promptly arrested and taken to Cannon Row police station.

The hour that followed will long be remembered in London. At intervals of fifteen minutes, relays of women who had volunteered for the demonstration did their work. The first smashing of glass occurred in the Haymarket and Piccadilly [important sections of London, the British capital]. These incidents greatly startled and alarmed both people passing by and the police. A large number of the women were arrested. Everybody thought this would end the affair.

However, before the police had reached the station with their prisoners, the smashing of plate glass began again. This time it was along both sides of Regent Street and the Strand. A furious rush of police and people toward the second scene of action followed. While their attention was being taken up in this quarter, the third relay of women began breaking the windows in Oxford and Bond Streets. The demonstration ended for the day at half past six with the breaking of many windows.

Something like two hundred suffragettes were taken to the various police stations. For days, long processions of women streamed through the courts. When these women were charged, they made clear statements of their motives. One of the prisoners said, "We have tried every means—processions and meetings—which did not get results. We have tried demonstrations, and now, at last, we have to break windows. I wish I had broken more. I am not in the least sorry. What is the good of a country like ours? You only have one point of view, and that is the men's. While men have done the best they could, they cannot go far without the women and the women's views."

Adapted from Emmeline Pankhurst, *My Own Story.* Hearst's International Library.

These workmen are replacing a London store window that has been broken by suffragettes. What do you think they hoped to accomplish by breaking windows?

▶ THINKING IT THROUGH

1. This article describes a campaign of the militant suffragettes.
   a. What reasons do they give for breaking windows?
   b. Do you approve of their actions? Why or why not?
2. During World War I, British women performed many services for the armed forces and did many jobs formerly reserved for men. Do you think these services helped women gain the vote? Explain.
3. There is an active women's liberation movement in the United States today. Women are demanding greater political, economic, and social power. Do you approve of this movement? Why or why not?

10. HOW HAS THE HOUSE OF LORDS BEEN WEAKENED?

The House of Lords was another aspect of the British government where democratic practices were restricted. For hundreds of years the Lords represented the interests of a small but wealthy upper class. This class consisted of nobles who had inherited their titles and who owned large estates. The House of Lords was usually more powerful than the House of Commons. Also, many members of the Lords controlled enough votes in their districts to have their supporters elected to Commons.

During modern times, the power of the House of Lords has been greatly reduced. You have already seen (in selection 7) how the prime minister forced the Lords to pass the Reform Bill of 1832. He threatened to "pack" the Lords with sympathizers. By using the same threat, the prime minister and the Commons later forced the House of Lords to pass laws limiting its own powers. The next selection tells how the House of Lords was weakened. It also shows what powers English noblemen still enjoy today.

A BLOW TO THE LORDS

It was the [House of] Lords that laid the basis for British democracy by forcing King John to accept Magna Carta in 1215. In the 14th century, the Lords began to share their Parliamentary power with the Commons, but they nonetheless managed to remain the dominant house until the

19th century. Three times in the 20th century British governments have significantly changed the Lords. Its power to delay legislation [laws] passed by the House of Commons was cut to two years in 1911 and cut again in 1949 to a single year. In 1958 the Tories [Conservatives] created life peerages permitting men and women of proved experience and distinction in such fields as science and education to be named peers [lords] without the privilege of passing on their titles.

Today the House of Lords has a membership of 1,045. . . . Its hereditary peers number 865. Twenty-six bishops of the Church of England sit as lords spiritual, and 154 life peers have been created. . . . In a title-conscious country, the Lords enjoy high prestige. Their most important perquisite [privilege] is to sit in the . . . House of Lords. . . . [A well-known writer notes,] "A Lord finds it easier to get servants, to run up credit, to get the best cuts of beef, to book tables at restaurants. . . ."

Defenders of the role of the Lords in British political life make some persuasive arguments. Being politically independent, the peers can take a broader view on public policy than M. P.'s [literally "members of Parliament," but actually refers to members of Commons]. The Lords bring to their debates . . . authority in education, culture, and travel. Moreover, they have more leisure to examine important public questions at searching length. . . .

Opposing speakers arguing a point before the House of Commons. For what reasons is debate important to parliamentary government?

Reprinted by permission from *Time, The Weekly Newsmagazine;* Copyright Time Inc. November 10, 1967.

▶ **THINKING IT THROUGH**

1. This article reports that "life peerages" were created in 1958.
   a. What are life peerages?
   b. How do they weaken the position of the hereditary nobles?
2. The power of the House of Lords has been weakened in other ways.
   a. In what ways has it been weakened?
   b. What powers do the Lords still have today?
3. English peers still enjoy certain privileges today.
   a. What are these privileges?
   b. Is it democratic for the peers to have these privileges? Explain.
4. Do you think the House of Lords should be further weakened or even abolished? Explain.

11. HOW DOES THE BRITISH GOVERNMENT WORK TODAY?

Great Britain is known as "the mother of parliaments." This is because many of its former colonies and a number of other countries have adopted its parliamentary system of government. The diagram below shows you how the British government works. After examining the diagram carefully, look over selections 5–7. Then answer the questions below the diagram.

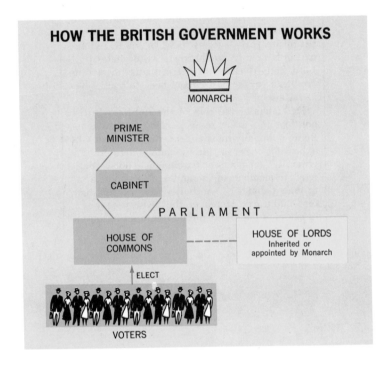

HOW THE BRITISH GOVERNMENT WORKS

MONARCH

PRIME MINISTER

CABINET

PARLIAMENT

HOUSE OF COMMONS

HOUSE OF LORDS
Inherited or appointed by Monarch

↑ ELECT

VOTERS

▶ INTERPRETING THE DIAGRAM

1. Who is the effective leader of the British government? Explain your choice.
2. What bodies does Parliament consist of? Which is more important? Explain.
3. "The House of Commons is *directly* responsible to the people, but the prime minister and cabinet are responsible to the people *indirectly.*" Explain.
4. In what ways do persons become members of the House of Lords?

Reviewing Chapter 1

SUMMING UP

1. This chapter describes the steps by which democracy has developed in Great Britain since 1215.
   a. What are these steps?
   b. Which step do you consider the most important one? Why?

2. It is said that Great Britain achieved democracy by evolution. Explain this statement.

3. Is the British government today democratic—that is, does it express its people's wishes? Support your answer.

FOR FURTHER INQUIRY

1. "In a democracy, the minority has its say, but the majority has its way."
   a. Explain the two parts of the above statement.
   b. Does the statement accurately describe British democracy? Explain.
   c. Is it also true of the United States today? Support your answer.

2. Which do you consider more important, Magna Carta or the Reform Act of 1832? Why?

3. As a result of the several Reform Acts, "the new wine of democracy was poured into the old bottle, Parliament."
   a. What does this mean?
   b. Would it have been better to reshape Parliament in order to make it more democratic? Explain.

4. "Few shall have more than they need, and fewer still shall have less than they need."
   a. Do you approve of this slogan of the British Labour Party? Why or why not?
   b. Did the measures the British government adopted to improve conditions for the working people (on pages 15–16) also make the country more democratic? Explain.

5. Give the arguments for or against each of the following questions:
   a. Should the British monarchy be abolished?
   b. Should the House of Lords be abolished?
   c. Should the United States President be made responsible to Congress in the way that the British prime minister is responsible to Parliament?

ROLE-PLAYING: DRAMATIZATION

Be prepared to take part in a short play in which the class acts as the House of Commons discussing an important current problem. Choose either the role of the prime minister, a member of his cabinet, or a leading member of the opposition. At the end of the discussion, the House of Commons should vote on the issue. If the prime minister is defeated, he should either resign or dismiss the Commons. Before taking either action, however, he should give the reasons for his decision.

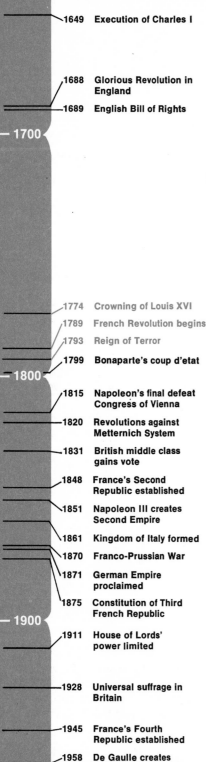

CHAPTER **2**

How Did the French People Overthrow Absolutism?

British democracy developed gradually, step by step. Though there was some violence and bloodshed, most of the growth was peaceful. The French arrived at democracy from a different path. The French people shook off absolutism in a series of REVOLUTIONS (great changes, usually made by force).

This chapter tells the story of the French Revolution. It began in 1789 and lasted ten years. France had four different governments during that period. This chapter shows why the French people overthrew their king. It also discusses why there were so many changes of government during this revolution.

22

1.

WHY DID THE FRENCH PEOPLE TURN AGAINST THEIR KINGS?

In an absolute monarchy, the country's peace and prosperity depended, to a large degree, on the person fate placed on the throne. This was because the absolute monarch enjoyed a great deal of power. Louis XIV, who ruled France from 1643 to 1715, was a typical absolute monarch. He left France in bad condition because of his wars and extravagance. His grandson, Louis XV (1715–1774), made matters worse. He was more interested in personal pleasure than in hard work. France lost several wars during his long reign. Taxes were raised time and again. But the royal treasury was almost always empty. Louis XV once said of his kingdom, "It will hold together as long as I live. Let my successor look out for himself." As this comment shows, he realized France might be headed toward serious difficulty.

Revolutionaries gather to swear an oath of brotherly love during the French Revolution. What purpose do you think such vows served?

King Louis XVI.

A strong and able monarch might still have saved the French throne. The next ruler, however, was LOUIS XVI (1774–1792), a person of ordinary ability. His main interests were in hunting and clock-repairing, rather than political affairs. He wanted to improve conditions, but was easily persuaded to change his plans. He was especially influenced by his wife, MARIE ANTOINETTE. The queen was a bubbly, pleasure-seeking young woman. She was very extravagant and interfered in government affairs to please her friends. The French people liked Louis. They blamed "that Austrian woman," as they called the queen, for his mistakes.

Early in his reign, Louis appointed two popular ministers. They planned to cut the court's expenses and make other reforms. But the courtiers complained to the queen, who persuaded the king to dismiss these able men. The next selection is part of a letter written to Marie Antoinette by her mother, the empress of Austria. The Austrian ruler warns her daughter to behave better. Do you think Marie Antoinette took her mother's advice?

Queen Marie Antoinette and her children.

I am very glad that you had nothing to do with the dismissal of the two ministers. They enjoy a high reputation with the general public. In my opinion, their only mistake was in trying to do too much at once. You say that you are not sorry they were dismissed. You undoubtedly have good reasons for your opinion. Lately, however, the public no longer praises you as it did. It blames you for all sorts of behavior that would be most unfitting to your position. The king loves you, and his ministers should respect you. By not acting against the general welfare, you will make yourself both loved and respected.

My only fear for you, because you are so young, is too much love of pleasure. You have never cared to read or to apply yourself in any way. This has often troubled me. It is the reason I have bothered you so often with questions about what you were reading. I was so pleased to see you devoting yourself to music. But for a year now there has been no question of either reading or music. I hear of nothing but racing and hunting. You are always without the king and with a lot of ill-chosen young people.

All this troubles me very much, loving you dearly as I do. These wild pleasures in which the king takes no part appear to me improper. You will say, "He knows and approves of them." I reply that he is kind and good. That is all the more reason that you should be careful and arrange your pleasures together.

Adapted from J. H. Robinson and C. A. Beard, *Readings in Modern European History,* pp. 239–240.

▶ THINKING IT THROUGH

1. In this letter the empress of Austria criticizes the way her daughter has been behaving.
   a. Do you think the advice was good?
   b. Would you expect Marie Antoinette to follow it?
   Explain each answer.
2. Louis XVI and Marie Antoinette could not cope with the difficulties of ruling France in the latter part of the eighteenth century.
   a. Do you think they would have been satisfactory rulers in a less difficult time? Explain.
   b. Why were they not fit to rule France in a time of troubles? Explain.
   c. What weakness of absolute monarchy does this situation show?

2. WHY WERE THE PEASANTS DISSATISFIED?

Revolution often breaks out in a country when conditions are so bad that the people desperately want a change. Some of the troubles that led to revolution in eighteenth-century France had existed for a long time. These troubles are known as the evils, or abuses, of the OLD REGIME (the old order).

Instead of reforming these abuses, Louis XV and Louis XVI allowed them to grow worse. The next selection describes the bad economic conditions in France. It was written by Arthur Young, an Englishman who traveled through France from 1787 to 1789. Why were the difficulties he describes among the basic causes of the French Revolution?

August 4, 1787

In this journey, I have passed a great number of splendid bridges and many superb roads. This only proves the foolishness of the government. These splendid bridges and large roads cannot be made merely for the use of the people who live here. One-fourth of the expense would be enough for useful travel. These things are therefore objects of public display. They are meant for the eye of travelers.

Public works are usually done by the *corvée* system. In this system, the peasants of the area are required to do several days' work each year without pay. In the south of France, money is raised by the *taille*. This is a tax on the land and its produce. There is an injustice in levying the amount each person must pay. Lands held by the nobility are taxed very little. Lands held by commoners are taxed heavily.

August 23, 1787

We passed a rich and highly cultivated valley on the way to Aiguillon. I saw the castle of the duke of Aiguillon. It was begun about twenty years ago. At that time, the duke was exiled here for eight years [from the royal court]. Thanks to that banishment, the building went on very well. However, as soon as the sentence was reversed, the duke went back to Paris. He has not been here since. As a result, all stands still. It is thus that banishment alone will force the French nobility to do what the English do for pleasure—live on and take care of their estates.

October 14, 1787

We came to the abbey [monastery] of St. Germain. It is the richest abbey in France. The abbot [head of the abbey] receives 300,000 livres [about $1.5 million] a year. I lose my patience at such revenues being granted in this manner. What a noble farm one-fourth of this income would establish! What turnips, what potatoes, what sheep, what wool! Are not these things better than a fat clergyman?

September 5, 1788

We came to Montauban. The poor people seem poor, indeed. The children are terribly ragged. They are worse clad, if possible, than if they had no clothes at all. I saw a beautiful girl six or seven years old playing with a stick. She smiled under such a bundle of rags as made my heart ache to see her. One-third of what I have seen of this province seems uncultivated. Nearly all of it seems in misery.

July 1789

Walking up a long hill to rest my horse, I was joined by a poor woman who complained of the hard times. She said her husband had only a tiny piece of land, one cow, and a poor little horse. Yet they had to pay 42 pounds of wheat and three chickens as rent to one noble. They also paid 168 pounds of oats and one chicken to another noble, besides very heavy *tailles* and other taxes. "The *tailles* and feudal dues [rents owed the lords since feudal times] are crushing us," she said. This woman, at no great distance, might have been taken for sixty or seventy years old. Her figure was bent, and her face was wrinkled and hardened by labor. However, she said she was only twenty-eight.

The *capitaineries* [hunting reserves] are another curse on all the people who occupy the land. These reserves are districts granted by the king to princes of the royal blood. The princes own all the game in these districts, even on lands not belonging to them. Game means whole droves of wild boars and herds of deer that are not confined by any wall or fence. The animals wander at pleasure over the whole country, destroying the crops. The game in a single reserve did damage to the amount of 184,263 livres [almost $1 million] a year. No wonder that we find people saying, "We loudly demand the destruction of the *capitaineries* and of all sorts of game."

They also ask, as a favor, to be allowed to "harvest their grain, mow their meadows, and remove the leftover stalks without regard to partridges [a bird] and other game." There are many laws for preserving game. These laws forbid weeding and hoeing, which might disturb the young partridges. Mowing hay before a certain time, so late as to spoil the crop, and taking away the stalks are also forbidden. These harvest activities would take away the birds' shelter.

Adapted from Arthur Young, *Travels in France*, 1794.

▶ **THINKING IT THROUGH**

1. This passage describes the evils of the Old Regime.
   a. What are these evils?
   b. Which do you consider the worst ones? Why?
2. What difference does Arthur Young note between the English and the French nobility? Was the difference an important one? Explain.
3. If you had been a peasant in eighteenth-century France, would you have supported a revolt against the king? Why or why not?

3. WHY WERE THE CLERGY AND NOBLES CALLED "THE PRIVILEGED CLASSES"?

One of the main evils of the Old Regime was the existence of PRIVILEGED CLASSES. (These are groups in society whose members enjoy special consideration because of their rank or power.) In eighteenth-century France, the clergy and the nobility still held special rights they had gained during the Middle Ages. They owned a great deal of land, as the chart on page 28 shows. They collected rent from the peasants on their land. They had the right to collect certain taxes besides. They also held the highest positions in the government and often received pensions from the king. Despite their large income, they did not have to pay certain royal taxes, such as the *taille*.

To understand why the common people disliked the privileged classes, look at the chart. Then answer the questions under the chart.

THE THREE ESTATES IN 1789

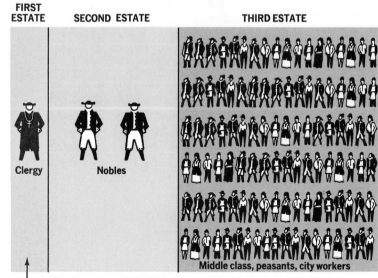

FIRST ESTATE **SECOND ESTATE** **THIRD ESTATE**

Clergy Nobles Middle class, peasants, city workers

2% of the people owned 35% of the land   97% of the people owned 55% of the land

1% of the people owned 10% of the land

▶INTERPRETING THE CHART

1. Name the two privileged classes in France during the Old Regime.
2. What percentage of the population did each privileged class represent? What percentage did both represent together?
3. What percentage of the land did each privileged class own? What percentage did both own together?
4. What group of people was considered as the commoners?
5. What percentage of the population was considered as the common people? What percentage of the land did this group own?
6. Based on this chart, what was the relation of land ownership to class privilege in France during the Old Regime?

4. HOW DID THE REVOLUTION BEGIN?

The evils of the Old Regime were the basic, or fundamental, causes of the French Revolution. These evils had existed for a long time. But the French people had become more and more unwilling to bear them. The immediate cause of the Revolution was the fact that the French government was bankrupt—that is, it could not meet its expenses. Bankers refused to lend it money, even at 40 percent interest a year! To make matters worse, France suffered from a bad harvest and a very cold winter in 1788. Starving people fled from the countryside to the cities, where they expected the government to feed them.

To meet this emergency, Louis XVI called up an old representative assembly, the Estates-General. He asked it to approve new taxes. The Estates-General consisted of three groups—one representing the clergy, the second the nobility, and the third the common people. Each body, known as an *estate*, had one vote. So the first two estates, the privileged classes, could outvote the commoners two to one.

As soon as the Estates-General met, the leaders of the Third Estate put forth their demands on the voting procedure. They wanted all three groups to meet together and each representative to have one vote. Such a system would be based on individual numbers and not on classes. It would give the commoners a majority. Louis XVI refused their demands. He sent troops to drive the Third Estate from its meeting place. However, the deputies defied him. They took an oath not to disband until they had their way. The king gave in. The Estates-General now became a single body. It was renamed the NATIONAL ASSEMBLY to show that it represented the whole French nation. This was the beginning of the French Revolution.

The National Assembly promised to draw up a constitution making France a limited monarchy. What would you expect Louis XVI to do about that? To find out what happened next, read the following account by the English traveler Arthur Young.

Representatives of the people voting to defy the king's order to disband. What voting method are they using?

Paris, June 10, 1789

Everything makes the present period in France critical. The lack of bread is terrible. Stories arrive every moment from the provinces of riots and of calling in soldiers to keep order in the markets. The price of bread has risen above the people's ability to pay. This causes great misery.

Paris, June 11, 1789

Yesterday the Abbé Siéyès [a former priest] made a motion in the Third Estate. He boldly declared that if the privileged classes would not join the Third Estate, it would meet without them. The house voted his motion. This caused much talk about what would be the result of such an action.

Versailles, June 15, 1789

This has been a rich day. Ten years ago no one would have believed it could ever arrive in France. A very important debate was expected on the state of the nation. My friend and I were at Versailles by eight in the morning. We went immediately to the hall to get good seats in the gallery. We found some deputies, as well as a pretty large audience already there. The large size of the room gave dignity to the scene. Representatives of 25 million people, just emerging from two hundred years of absolute rule, were assembled with open doors under the eye of the public.

There are, however, two ways in which their proceedings are very poor. The first weakness is that the people watching from the galleries are allowed to interfere in the debates. They can clap their hands and make other noisy expressions of approval. This behavior is disrespectful. It is also dangerous. If they are allowed to show approval, they are also allowed to show disagreement. The other weakness is the lack of order among the members. More than once today a hundred rose to their feet at one time. The president of the Assembly was absolutely powerless to keep order.

A mob attempting to break into the king's palace. The man standing in front of the window is the mob's leader. What do you think he is saying?

A Paris mob storming the Bastille, a prison where political prisoners were kept. The soldiers joined the people in the attack instead of holding them off. Why do you think they did so?

Metz, July 14, 1789

The news from Paris is interesting. Versailles and Paris are surrounded by troops. Thirty-five thousand men are assembled and 20,000 more are on the road. The assembling of such a number of troops has added to the scarcity of bread. The confusion and lack of order in the capital are extreme. A civil war seems certain.

Strasbourg, July 20, 1789

On arriving at an inn, I heard the interesting news of the revolt of Paris. The French Guards joined the people in taking the Bastille [the king's prison]. A bourgeois militia [middle-class police force] was set up. In a word, the old government has been overthrown. Everything is now being decided. The kingdom is in the hands of the National Assembly. They have the power to make a new constitution. It will be a great sight for the world to view. The representatives of 25 million people will be building a new and better form of liberty than Europe has yet offered.

Adapted from Arthur Young, *Travels in France*, 1794.

▶ THINKING IT THROUGH

1. How did the shortage of bread early in 1789 help start the Revolution?
2. Why was the National Assembly able to defeat the king, even though he brought a large army to Versailles?
3. Why is Bastille Day, July 14, celebrated by the French as a national holiday?
4. Do you think Louis XVI could have prevented the Revolution? Explain.

5. HOW DID THE NATIONAL ASSEMBLY CHANGE THE OLD REGIME?

The National Assembly remained in power for two years (1789–1791). Then it issued the constitution for a new government and went home. Its two most important actions are described below.

a. The Reforms of August 1789

The most sweeping reforms of the French Revolution were made at the very beginning of the National Assembly. Frightened by rioting in the provinces, the upper classes suddenly agreed to give up most of their privileges. This dramatic scene is described below by an eyewitness.

During the evening, a member of the National Assembly read a proclamation. This announcement had been prepared to stop the attacks on the nobles' castles. It ordered the payment of taxes, rents, and feudal dues, which the people were refusing to pay. This led to a great debate. It was pointed out that the peasants were refusing to pay feudal dues and were burning feudal title deeds. They were doing these things because they hated the feudal regime and the burdens it placed on them.

At this point, the viscount of Noailles [a nobleman] made a motion that taxes should be borne equally by all. The *corvees* [forced labor] should be abolished. Peasants should have the right to pay their feudal dues in cash. The duke of Aiguillon added that all privileges should be done away with. The duke of Chatelet asked that all tithes [church taxes] should be payable in cash [instead of in farm products]. The bishop of Chartres asked for the end of the hunting rights. Many other nobles, one by one, gave up their feudal rights. For centuries the feudal regime had weighed most heavily on the people. It was now destroyed by a single stroke.

Adapted from J. B. Duvergier (ed.), *Collection complete des lois* (Vol. I), Paris, 1834, pp. 33–34.

▶ THINKING IT THROUGH

1. Why did the peasants burn the feudal title deeds?
2. Why did the nobles agree to give up their feudal rights?

3. Suppose the nobles had given up their privileges sooner. Do you think the French Revolution might have been avoided? Explain.

b. The Declaration of the Rights of Man

The constitution drawn up by the National Assembly provided that the new government would be a limited monarchy. This constitution included a complete bill of rights called the DECLARATION OF THE RIGHTS OF MAN. *The American Bill of Rights was adopted at about the same time (in 1791). Would you expect the two documents to be similar?*

The Declaration of the Rights of Man. What rights do you think should be included in such a document?

The representatives of the French people have acted as a National Assembly. They have decided to set forth in a solemn declaration the natural, inalienable [not to be taken away], and sacred rights of man.

Men are born and remain free and equal in rights.

The aim of all government is to protect the natural rights of man. These rights are of liberty, property, and security, and to resist oppression.

Liberty is the freedom to do all that does not harm others.

The law has the right to forbid only those actions harmful to society.

Law is the expression of the general will. All citizens have the right to assist personally, or by their representatives, in the making of the law. It should be the same for all. All citizens are to be equally admitted to all public positions and employments according to their ability.

No man can be accused, arrested, or held prisoner except in cases decided by law.

Every man is considered innocent until he has been declared guilty. All harsh treatment not necessary for holding the prisoner should be prevented by law.

No person should be disturbed because of his opinions, even in religion, provided he does not disturb the public order.

To freely express thoughts and opinions is one of the most precious rights of man. Every citizen can speak, write, and publish freely.

Taxes ought to be equally distributed among all citizens according to their means.

Property is a sacred right that cannot be violated. No one's property can be taken away except when public need clearly demands it. Then it can only be taken on payment of a fair price.

Adapted from J. B. Duvergier (ed.), *Collection complete des lois* (Vol. III), Paris, 1834, p. 240.

▶ THINKING IT THROUGH

1. ''Liberty, Equality, Fraternity'' was a slogan of the French Revolution.
   a. Which parts of the Declaration of the Rights of Man protected the liberty of the French people?
   b. Which parts gave them equality?
      Explain in each instance.
2. Based on this document, how should citizens of a democracy contribute to lawmaking?
3. Why was the Declaration of the Rights of Man important—not only for France but also for other European countries?

6. HOW DID THE FRENCH PEOPLE FIGHT THE KINGS OF EUROPE?

The new government was known as the Legislative (lawmaking) Assembly. Unfortunately, this body proved too weak and inexperienced to deal with the many problems France faced. One problem was the bitter opposition of the upper classes. Many nobles fled to neighboring countries and begged foreign rulers to invade France. Marie Antoinette secretly asked her brother, the Austrian emperor, to lead the invasion. The king and queen tried to flee from France, but were caught. The Legislative Assembly then declared war on Austria. Prussia (a large state in Germany), Britain, Spain, and Holland later joined in the fighting. At the same time, revolts led by supporters of the French monarchy took place within France.

The king and queen (in the coach) being brought back to Paris after attempting to flee from France. How do you think the people felt about this incident?

a. Mobilizing the People

Faced with civil and foreign wars, the French government was taken over by new leaders. They arrested the king and queen, and made France a republic. The new republic was ruled by a body called the NATIONAL CONVENTION. *The Convention took prompt, strong action. One of its measures was a law creating a military draft. This was the first such law in modern history. Compare this draft law with the laws some nations have today. Why do you think the French law was so far-reaching in the demands it made on the French people?*

In this bloody street battle, workers and soldiers defeated the king's guards. They then arrested the king and his family. Why do you think the revolutionaries felt it necessary to take this action?

1. All Frenchmen are permanently drafted for the service of the armies. This shall be true from this moment until the enemy has been driven from the territory of the republic.

   The young men shall go to battle. The married men shall make weapons and transport supplies. The women shall make tents and clothing, and shall serve in hospitals. The children shall make old linen into bandages. The old men shall go to the public places. There they shall arouse the courage of the warriors. They shall preach hatred of kings and the unity of the republic.

2. The public buildings shall be used as barracks [living quarters for the soldiers]. The public squares shall become workshops to make arms.

3. Arms powerful enough for military use shall be kept solely for those who shall march upon the enemy. The military forces needed within France [the militia] shall be provided with hunting pieces and side arms.

4. Saddle horses shall be taken to equip the cavalry. Workhorses, other than those used in agriculture, shall haul the artillery and the provisions.

5. The Committee of Public Safety [a small group of officials chosen by the Convention] is charged with taking all necessary measures to establish an extraordinary manufacture of arms of every kind. It shall form all the establishments, workshops, and mills necessary for these works. It shall also call into service the craftsmen and other workingmen who can contribute to the success of these operations.

6. The representatives of the people sent to carry out the present law shall have unlimited powers.

7. Nobody can have a substitute for himself in the service for which he has been drafted. Civil service [government] employees shall remain at their posts.

8. The levy shall be general. The unmarried citizens and widowers without children, from eighteen to twenty-five years of age, shall march first. They shall gather without delay at the main towns of their districts. There they shall practice every day in the use of arms while awaiting the hour of departure.

Adapted from George L. Mosse et al (eds.), *Europe in Review*, Rev., © 1957, 1964 by Rand McNally and Company, Chicago, pp. 170–171.

▶ THINKING IT THROUGH

1. Why did the Convention adopt such an extreme draft law?
2. The Convention gave the Committee of Public Safety unlimited powers.
   a. Why did the Convention take this step?
   b. Was it wise to do so? Explain.
3. Would you expect the new citizen army of France to fight better than the hired soldiers of the kings of Europe? Why or why not?

b. The Importance of the "Marseillaise"

A strong feeling of patriotism, of love for one's nation, is called NATIONALISM. *Before the French Revolution, people generally thought of themselves as subjects of a certain king or as inhabitants of a certain district. During the Revolution, however, the representatives of the French people took power from the king. To show that they represented the French nation, they called themselves the* National Assembly *and the* National Convention. *Their citizen armies, marching into battle against foreign invaders, strengthened the new feeling of nationalism. Note how this feeling was also expressed in the French marching song, written in the city of Marseilles. The "Marseillaise" is still the French national anthem today.*

Arise, children of the fatherland,
Our day of glory has arrived.
Against us cruel tyrants
Have raised their bloody flag.
Do you hear in the countryside
Their fierce hired soldiers?
They come almost into your arms
To attack your children and your fields.

CHORUS

To arms, citizens!
Form your battalions!
March on, march on,
To liberty or death!

Translated by Sidney Schwartz from the original song by Rouget de Lisle.

▶ INTERPRETING THE SONG

1. How does the "Marseillaise" appeal to nationalism? Quote from the song to support your answer.
2. Why does war often strengthen a people's feeling of nationalism?
3. "It is better to die on your feet than to live on your knees."
   a. Explain this statement, which was popular among American and British soldiers during World War II.
   b. How does it show the same type of nationalist feeling that the "Marseillaise" does?

7. WHAT WAS THE REIGN OF TERROR?

The new citizen armies of France succeeded in driving back the foreign invaders. But fighting continued for years. The fear of National defeat caused the government to move in an extreme direction. A group called the JACOBINS gained control of the

Convention and the Committee of Public Safety. The Jacobins were RADICALS. They wanted to uproot the old order and build a new society. They wanted to help the workers and to give them equal rights with the middle class. Under the leadership of the Jacobins, the Convention gave the vote to all men. It ended the old custom of throwing people into jail if they owed money. It also divided the estates of the nobles and clergy among the peasants.

The fear that war would undo the revolution led to the REIGN OF TERROR. The government took extreme measures designed to rid the republic of its enemies. The king and queen were brought to trial for treason and executed. Many of the nobility were killed as well. The execution of large numbers of commoners followed. Finally, discredited members of the Convention were put to death.

Altogether, some twenty thousand people were killed. Most of them were beheaded by a newly-invented instrument, the guillotine. The selection below describes a typical scene during the Reign of Terror.

The victims were lined up with their backs to the guillotine so they would not have to see what it was like. All forty-five were put in line. Then the executioner drew a blood-stained smock over his clothes. He gave a signal to his two assistants. They seized the first victim and half lifted him up the steps to the scaffold. The executioner held him by the right arm. The assistant held him by the left arm. The third man took him by the feet. In an instant, the man was thrown against the plank onto his stomach. There were three dull thuds—that of the plank going forward, that of the neck clamp falling into place, and that of the axe falling. The man's body and head were tossed into the large straw-lined cart. The whole business took less than two minutes.

Condemned prisoners being led to the guillotine during the Reign of Terror. What do you think the Terror government hoped to achieve by such gory public executions?

The assistants seized the second victim. They did away with him with the same quick efforts. The wife of the marshall of Noailles was the third to mount this altar. It was necessary to cut the upper part of the neck of her dress to expose her throat. Mme. d'Ayen was tenth in line. When she mounted the scaffold, the executioner pulled off her bonnet. It was fastened by a pin which he did not trouble to take out. The pain of having her hair pulled was evident in her expression. Then she too died. Her daughter, dressed all in white and looking far younger than her years, followed. The same thing happened in her case as in her mother's. The same oversight as to the pin, the same pain, the same calm, the same death!

Adapted from the book *Paris in the Terror: June 1793–July 1794*, by Stanley Loomis. Copyright © 1964 by Stanley Loomis. Reprinted by permission of J. B. Lippincott Company.

▶ **THINKING IT THROUGH**

1. The Convention made many changes in France.
   a. How did it strengthen the idea of equality?
   b. Did it also strengthen the idea of liberty? Explain.
2. The guillotine was considered more humane than the headsman's axe or the hangman's noose. Do you agree? Why or why not?
3. Crowds came to watch the early executions, but few people attended the later ones. Why do you think this happened?
4. Do you think conditions in France justified the Reign of Terror? Explain.

8. WHAT WERE THE STAGES OF THE FRENCH REVOLUTION?

The Reign of Terror ended when the most powerful man in the Convention, the Jacobin leader Maximilien Robespierre, was himself executed. Still another new government, called the Directory, was then set up. The Directory promised to bring peace, unity, and prosperity to France. It failed to do so and was overthrown by a military commander, Napoleon Bonaparte.

Altogether, the French Revolution lasted ten years, from 1789 to 1799. During that time, four governments held power and many important reforms were made. Study the chart on page 40, which presents an overall picture of the Revolution. Judging by the chart, did the Revolution create a more democratic nation?

Name of Government	Dates	Form of Government	Major Developments
National Assembly	1789–1791	Limited monarchy	Abolished most of the evils of the Old Regime. Issued the Declaration of the Rights of Man.
Legislative Assembly	1791–1792	Limited monarchy	Declared war on the kings of Europe.
National Convention	1792–1795	Republic	Raised a citizens' army to defend France. Strengthened the new feeling of nationalism. Allowed all men to vote. Divided the estates of the upper classes among the common people. Conducted the Reign of Terror against "enemies of the people."
Directory	1795–1799	Republic	Continued the European war. Appointed Bonaparte commander of the French Army in Italy.

▶ INTERPRETING THE CHART

1. Which of the four governments during the French Revolution made the most important changes? Explain your choice.
2. Which was the most revolutionary government? Explain.
3. In what basic ways was France in 1799 different from what it had been ten years earlier when the Revolution began?
4. Weigh the achievements of the French Revolution against its costs. Do you consider the Revolution worthwhile? Explain.

Reviewing Chapter 2

SUMMING UP

1. The word "political" refers to government, the way people are ruled. The word "economic" refers to the way people satisfy their material wants. The word "social" refers to the way people live together in groups or communities.
   a. What were the fundamental causes of the French Revolution?
   b. Which of these were political, which were economic, and which were social causes?
2. What was the *immediate* cause of the French Revolution? Explain the difference between fundamental and immediate causes.
3. What important changes were made in France during the Revolution. Which of them were political, economic, or social?

FOR FURTHER INQUIRY

1. Louis XV is reported to have said, "It [the French monarchy] will hold together as long as I live. Let my successor look out for himself."
   a. What did the king mean by this remark?
   b. Do you approve of his attitude? Why or why not?
2. The nobility was a privileged class in almost every European country in the eighteenth century.
   a. Why did many French people dislike their nobility?
   b. Why did many British people respect theirs?
   c. "Abuse of privilege, rather than privilege itself, was a basic cause of the French Revolution." Do you agree? Why or why not?
3. The phrase "too little, too late" has been used to describe Louis XVI's greatest weakness as a king.
   a. Do you agree with this opinion? Why or why not?
   b. Why is a king's personal character less important politically today than it was in the eighteenth century?
4. Independence Day is July 4 in the United States, July 14 in France.
   a. In what ways are the two holidays alike?
   b. What important difference was there in the way these holidays originated?
5. Most of the leaders of the French Revolution came from the middle class.
   a. Why do you think they came from this class?
   b. When the middle class came to power under the National Assembly, why did it want only moderate reforms?
   c. Why was the Convention, which was dominated by the city workers, more radical than the National Assembly?
6. The Declaration of the Rights of Man has been called "the death certificate of the Old Regime." Explain.
7. Compare the French Revolution that began in 1789 with the Glorious Revolution in England in 1688, by answering the following questions:
   a. What were the basic differences between the two revolutions?
   b. Which revolution was more successful? Support your answer.

ROLE-PLAYING

Be prepared to take part in a series of discussions concerning the French Revolution. Choose the role of a person from one of the classes of French society that are shown on the chart on page 28. You should be able to discuss the events in France, and how you feel about them, at each of the following times:
a. just before the Revolution.
b. under the National Assembly.
c. during the Reign of Terror.
d. just before Napoleon came to power.

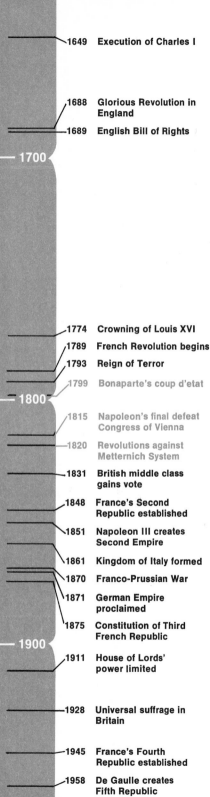

CHAPTER 3

How Were Revolutionary Ideas Spread Through Western Europe?

The slogan of "Liberty, Equality, Fraternity" expressed the main goals of the French Revolution. You have already seen how the revolutionary leaders proclaimed the principles of liberty and equality, and tried to put them into effect in France. They also sought to carry out the principle of fraternity ("brotherhood"). They tried to bring the new reforms to their "brothers," the common people in other countries.

This chapter describes how a bold young general named NAPOLEON BONAPARTE became the ruler of France. It shows how Bonaparte spread the ideas and reforms of the Revolution through most of Western Europe.

42

1. WHY DID GENERAL BONAPARTE BECOME FAMOUS?

Early in the Revolution, France went to war with the other leading European powers. These wars were still going on during the period of the Directory in France. This government put Bonaparte in command of the French army in Italy. General Bonaparte found the army in very bad condition. It lacked weapons, supplies, and discipline. He quickly got the forces into shape. Then he surprised all Europe by winning a series of brilliant victories over the Italian rulers and their ally, the emperor of Austria.

The following selection is a bulletin issued by General Bonaparte. It was meant to whip up the spirit of his soldiers. As you read it, look for reasons for his success.

A painting of Napoleon Bonaparte, done by an artist of the French Revolution. Judging from this painting, how do you think the artist felt about Napoleon?

In two weeks you have won six victories. You have taken twenty-one enemy flags and fifty-five pieces of artillery. You have captured 15,000 prisoners, and killed or wounded more than 10,000 men. Soldiers of liberty, only republican forces could have done what you have done. Soldiers, you have our thanks! Our nation is grateful to you.

But, soldiers, you have done nothing compared with what remains to be done. You still have battles to fight, cities to capture, rivers to cross. Is there one among you whose courage is weakening? No. All of you are filled with the desire to extend the glory of the French people. All of you long to defeat those proud kings who dare to think of placing us in chains. All of you desire to dictate a glorious peace, which will pay our nation for the great sacrifices it has made. All of you wish to be able to say with pride as you return to your villages, "I was with the victorious army of Italy!"

Friends, I promise you this conquest. But there is one condition you must swear to fulfill. You must respect the people whom you liberate. You must end the horrible looting done by scoundrels working for our enemies. Otherwise, you would not be the liberators of the people. Instead, you would be their scourge [whip].

Peoples of Italy, the French army comes to break your chains. The French people are the friend of all peoples. Come to us with confidence. Your property, your religion, and your customs will be respected.

We are waging war as generous enemies. We wish to crush the evil rulers who enslave you.

Adapted from John Hall Stewart, *A Documentary Survey of the French Revolution* (© Copyright, The Macmillan Company 1951), pp. 672–673.

▶ **THINKING IT THROUGH**

1. French troops did a great deal of looting at first.
   a. Why do you suppose they did this?
   b. What explanation does Napoleon give for the looting?
   c. Why do you think he gave this explanation?
2. In this speech what appeals does Napoleon make to his own troops? To the Italian people?
3. Why were Napoleon's speeches effective?

2. HOW DID BONAPARTE BECOME THE RULER OF FRANCE?

After his triumphs in Italy, Bonaparte led an expedition to Egypt. While he was away, other French commanders suffered serious defeats. Even more important, the Directory proved a very weak government. France's paper money became almost worthless. Business was upset and many people were thrown out of work. Discontent and disorder increased. People spoke of recalling a brother of Louis XVI to become king of France.

Bonaparte took advantage of this situation. Returning to Paris, he quickly seized power. (The sudden overthrow of a government by a small group of people is called a COUP D' ÉTAT.)

In taking power, Bonaparte first gained the support of the Directors and one house of the legislature, the Council of Elders. What happened when he tried to win over the other house, the Council of Five Hundred, is told in the two selections that follow. Which account do you think is more accurate?

Napoleon on horseback. What qualities do you think a military leader should have?

a. Bonaparte's Proclamation to the French People

The following version of the coup d'etat is the explanation Bonaparte gave the people of France.

Frenchmen! On my return to France I found division among all the authorities. They agreed only on the single point that the constitution was half destroyed and was unable to protect liberty.

Each party in turn came to me and requested my support. However, I refused to be the man of any party.

The Council of Elders appealed to me. I answered their appeal. They gave me the force necessary to protect them. I was bound by duty to accept the command. I was duty-bound to my fellow citizens, to the soldiers dying in our armies, and to the national glory gained at the cost of so much blood.

I went before the Council of Five Hundred alone, unarmed, my head uncovered. My object was to restore power to the majority of the Council. But twenty murderers rushed upon me and aimed their daggers at my breast. I had left soldiers at the door of the hall. They ran forward and placed themselves between me and the murderers. The soldiers took me out.

At the same moment, cries of "Outlaw him!" were raised against the defender of the law [Bonaparte]. The murderers crowded around the president of the Council [Napoleon's brother Lucien], making threats. With arms in their hands, they ordered him to declare me outlawed. I was informed of this. I ordered him to be rescued from their fury. I brought him out. Immediately afterwards, some soldiers charged the hall and cleared it.

The traitors fled. The majority returned freely and peaceably into the hall. They discussed the matter, then drew up the resolution which will become the new law of the republic.

Adapted from J. H. Robinson and C. A. Beard, *Readings in Modern European History*.

b. A Different View

The second account of what happened in the Council of Five Hundred was written years later by a brilliant French writer, Madame Germaine de Stael. She admired Napoleon at first, but later became one of his harshest critics.

He [Bonaparte] arrived in the Council of Five Hundred with his arms crossed and a very serious air. He was followed by two big soldiers, who protected his small person. The deputies called Jacobins shouted and howled on seeing him enter the room. His brother Lucien, fortunately for Bonaparte, was then president [of the Council]. Lucien rang the bell in vain to restore order. Cries of "Traitor" and "Usurper" were heard from every side. One of the deputies (a Corsican like

Napoleon) approached the general and seized him by the coat collar. It has been said, but without proof, that the deputy had a dagger to kill him. His action frightened Bonaparte. He told the soldiers at his side, *"Get me out of here."* The soldiers lifted him through the deputies and carried him out of the room.

After Bonaparte left, the deputies who were opposed to him demanded that he be declared an outlaw. It was then that his brother Lucien did Bonaparte a very great service. He refused, despite all the pressure on him, to put this proposal to a vote. If he had agreed, the decree would have passed. No one can tell now what effect this might have had on the soldiers.

Bonaparte soon sent an armed force to take Lucien to safety outside the Council. As soon as he had left, troops entered the room. They chased out the deputies by marching from one end of the room to the other, as if nobody were there. The deputies, pushed against the wall, were forced to flee by the window into the garden. This was the first time since the beginning of the revolution that the civilian government had been made to appear ridiculous by the military.

Adapted from Mme. de Stael, *Considerations sur les principaux evenements de la Revolution Francaise* (Charpentier, Editeur) 1845. (The passage used in the text was translated from the French by Sidney Schwartz.)

Mme. de Stael, the well-known French writer who opposed Napoleon.

▶ THINKING IT THROUGH

1. Compare the two versions of Bonaparte's coup d'etat, by answering the following questions:
   a. In what respects do the two accounts agree?
   b. In what respects do they differ?
   c. Which account seems more believable to you? Why?
2. In his version Bonaparte claimed that his life had been threatened by traitors.
   a. Why did he make this claim?
   b. Why did he pose as the defender of liberty?
3. Most French people accepted Bonaparte's seizure of power.
   a. Why did they support him?
   b. "What France needed in 1799 was not liberty, but order, efficiency, and victories." Do you agree with this statement? Why or why not?

3. *WHAT REFORMS DID BONAPARTE MAKE?*

Napoleon succeeded in giving the French people "order, efficiency, and victories." He quickly made a number of financial reforms that restored prosperity to France. He also made other reforms which, he claimed, preserved the principles of the French Revolution. Do you think his claim was well-founded?

During the very first night after he seized power, Napoleon appointed two committees to draft a legal code. This was the first act of his dictatorship! Until the outbreak of the Revolution, there had been no unified legal system in France. The Revolution brought the promise of such a system. But now, after eleven years, the promise was still not fulfilled. That first summer, three great lawyers were set to work. Four months later, a draft of the Civil Code, later renamed the NAPOLEONIC CODE, was ready. In eighteen months the new laws were voted.

This code is still the law of France. It was adopted in many of the lands conquered by Napoleon. Its influence later spread still farther afield to Central America and South America.

All that is new in the Napoleonic Code is drawn from the Revolution. There was no longer a hereditary nobility. All children had an equal share in inheritance. All parents became legally responsible for supporting their children. Jews became equal with Christians before the law. Civil marriage [marriage outside of the Catholic Church] became open to all. Also, it could be legally ended by divorce.

In his new education law, Napoleon established public elementary schools, high schools, and technical colleges throughout the country. There were to be six thousand free scholarships. The Ministry for Home Affairs drew up lists of "the ten best painters, sculptors, composers, musicians, architects, and other artists whose talents make them worthy of support" [by the government].

If there was to be no war and no court life, where would the French find an outlet for their vanity and ambition? Napoleon answered this question by founding the LEGION OF HONOR. The aim of this society was to provide distinctions for all who do good service to the nation.

Adapted from Emil Ludwig, *Napoleon*, 1954, pp. 170–171, 190.

▶ THINKING IT THROUGH

1. Napoleon considered the Code his greatest reform. Do you agree with him that it was very important? Why or why not?
2. Napoleon claimed that he was "a child of the Revolution."
   a. What do you think he meant by that?
   b. Was he actually a revolutionary himself? Explain.
3. Napoleon's reforms helped the French people. How did they also increase Napoleon's power?

4. HOW DID BONAPARTE BECOME AN ABSOLUTE MONARCH?

Napoleon's original title was First Consul. There were two other consuls, who supposedly shared power with him. But Napoleon quickly showed that he was the dictator of France. He abolished freedom of the press; he established a powerful secret police force. Five years later, in 1804, he crowned himself "Emperor of the French."

The following selection is part of the *Imperial Catechism*. This was a set of questions and answers that all school children in France were required to learn. What do you think was the purpose of this Catechism?

Question: What are the duties of Christians with respect to the princes who govern them? What in particular are our duties toward Napoleon I, our emperor?

Answer: Christians owe to the princes who govern them, and we owe in particular to Napoleon I, our emperor, *love*, respect, obedience, faithfulness, *military service*, and *taxes*. We also owe him prayers for his safety and for the prosperity of the state.

Question: Why are we bound to all these duties towards our emperor?

Answer: It is, first of all, because of God, who creates empires and distributes them according to His will. He has established our emperor as our ruler and has made him the minister of His power and His image on earth. *To honor and to serve our emperor is to honor and to serve God himself.*

Question: Are there not special reasons that ought to attach us more strongly to Napoleon I, our emperor?

Answer: Yes. He has restored and preserved public order by his great and active wisdom. He defends the state with his powerful arm. He has become the chosen of the Lord through the consecration [sacred ceremony] which he received from the Pope.

Question: What ought to be thought of those who are lacking in duty towards our emperor?

Answer: According to the apostle St. Paul, they would be resisting the order established by God Himself. They would make themselves *worthy of damnation forever.*

Question: Will the duties to which we are held towards our emperor be equally binding with respect to those who will legally succeed him?

Answer: Yes, without doubt. We read in the Holy Scripture that God, Lord of heaven and earth, gives empires not only to one person in particular, but also to his family.

Adapted from George L. Mosse et al (eds.), *Europe in Review*, Rev., © 1957, 1964 by Rand McNally and Company, Chicago, pp. 179–180.

Napoleon as emperor of the French. In making himself emperor Napoleon dissolved the government created by the French Revolution. If you had been a member of the Revolution, what would have been your reaction?

▶ **THINKING IT THROUGH**

1. Napoleon got the idea for his Imperial Catechism from the Catholic Church.
   a. How can you tell that the Church was the source for the Catechism?
   b. Why did he expect the Catechism to strengthen his authority as emperor?
2. "I found the crown of France lying in the gutter. I picked it up with my sword." Explain this statement by Napoleon.
3. In what ways was Napoleon's rule undemocratic?
4. Why did many Frenchmen accept Napoleon as their ruler?

5. HOW POWERFUL DID NAPOLEON BECOME?

When he first came to power, Napoleon made peace with the enemies of France. After he became emperor, however, he fought one war after another. Study the map below, then decide how successful he was.

EUROPE IN 1810

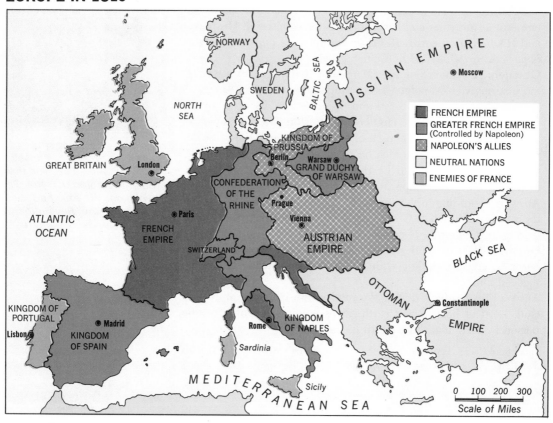

▶ INTERPRETING THE MAP

1. What territories other than the French Empire proper were under Napoleon's control?
2. Which powerful countries were his allies?
3. Napoleon claimed that he was the master of half of Europe. Do you agree with this claim? Why or why not?
4. Who were Napoleon's enemies in 1810? Who were the neutrals?

In this bloody battle, the armies of Prussia and Russia are fighting to stop Napoleon's invasion of Prussia. What do you think you would have done if Napoleon's armies had invaded your country?

6. *WHY WAS NAPOLEON DEFEATED?*

At first, people in other countries welcomed Napoleon as a liberator. By introducing the reforms of the French Revolution, he swept away the evils of the Old Regime. In later years, however, the people of the "liberated" countries began to turn against him. They objected to his use of their young men in his armies. He also increased taxes to pay for his wars. Another factor that helped arouse the people against Napoleon was the spirit of nationalism.

The following passage, written by a German historian, describes the rise of nationalism in Prussia. How did this spirit contribute to Napoleon's three great defeats—in Spain, in Russia, and in Prussia?

Fired with enthusiasm, the people rose "with God, for King and Fatherland." Among the Prussians there was only one voice, one feeling, one anger, and one love. They wanted to save the fatherland and to free Germany. The Prussians wanted war—war and death. They feared peace because they could hope for no honorable peace from Napoleon.

"War!" cried the nobleman who had been made poor. "War!" cried the peasant who was driving his last horse to death. "War!" cried the citizen who was exhausted from housing soldiers and paying taxes. "War!" cried the widow who was sending her only son to the front. "War!" cried the young girl who, with tears of pride and pain, was saying farewell to the man she was going to marry. One saw youths who were hardly able to bear arms, men with gray hair, and officers who on account of wounds had long ago been discharged. There were fathers of large families, and managers of important businesses. All were unwilling to remain behind. Even young women, under all sorts of disguises, rushed to arms.

All wanted to drill, arm themselves, and fight and die for the fatherland. All differences of position, class, and age were forgotten. The one great feeling for the fatherland, for its freedom and honor, swallowed all other feelings.

Adapted from Ernst M. Arndt, *Das preussische Volk und Heer,* in *Documents of German History,* translated by Louis L. Snyder. By permission of Rutgers University Press.

▶ THINKING IT THROUGH

1. Why did the German people turn against Napoleon, whom they had once welcomed as a liberator? Refer to the passage for facts to support your answer.
2. What evidence of the spirit of nationalism do you find in this passage? Give specific examples.
3. Napoleon had dreamed of uniting all Europe under his rule. Why did the rise of nationalism mean the end of his dream?

7. HOW DID NAPOLEON RETURN FOR "100 DAYS"?

After his enemies invaded France in 1814, Napoleon finally surrendered. He was exiled to Elba, a small island off the southern coast of France. He escaped, however, returned to Paris, and ruled for the next hundred days. Once again, the European powers united against him. He was defeated at Waterloo. This time he was sent off to St. Helena, a tropical island in the middle of the South Atlantic Ocean. There he died a few years later.

The following headlines from a French newspaper trace Napoleon's path after his escape from Elba. What do these reports reveal about the French attitude toward him?

THE CORSICAN MONSTER HAS LANDED IN THE GULF OF JUAN

THE CANNIBAL IS MARCHING TOWARD GRASSE

THE USURPER HAS ENTERED GRENOBLE

BONAPARTE HAS ENTERED LYONS

NAPOLEON IS MARCHING TOWARD FONTAINEBLEAU

HIS IMPERIAL MAJESTY IS EXPECTED TOMORROW IN PARIS

Napoleon's once Grand Army returning home from its defeat in Russia. How do you think the French people felt when they saw this sight?

▶ **THINKING IT THROUGH**

1. The tone of these headlines changes from the first one to the last.
   a. What attitude toward Napoleon is shown in the first three headlines? In the last three?
   b. How can you explain the difference?
2. What do these headlines indicate about the attitude of the French people toward Napoleon?
3. "If I give the French people glory, they will forget about liberty."
   a. How does this statement by Napoleon help to explain his many wars?
   b. Could Napoleon have prevented his downfall? Why or why not?
4. What were Napoleon's achievements while in power? What were his faults?
5. All things considered, do you think Napoleon was a great man? Explain.

8. HOW DID THE MONARCHS REMAKE EUROPE?

The leaders of the Congress of Vienna. They wished to make Europe the way it had been before the French Revolution. Why do you think this was not very realistic?

After defeating Napoleon, the rulers of Europe met to make the peace. Since the meeting was held at Vienna, the capital of the Austrian Empire, it is known as the CONGRESS OF VIENNA. Most rulers at the meeting were REACTIONARIES. They wanted to restore the conditions that existed before the French Revolution. They also wanted to make sure that France would not again threaten the rest of Europe.

As the first step toward achieving these purposes, the victors took away all the territories France had conquered. The main victorious powers were Great Britain, Russia, Austria, and Prussia. Each of them took some of these territories as payment for the losses it had suffered in the wars. In the remaining territories, the victors put back the rulers who had been driven out by the French. If a ruler had died, they put his heir on the throne as though it had never been vacant. This principle was carried out in France. Louis XVIII, brother of Louis XVI, was "restored" to the French throne even though he had never occupied it. Finally, the great powers formed a military agreement (a four-power alliance) to protect Europe against future uprisings.

Prince CLEMENS VON METTERNICH was chancellor (prime minister) of the Austrian Empire. He was also the most important leader at the Congress of Vienna. What does the following excerpt from his memoirs reveal about Metternich's attitude toward government by the people?

The governments have lost their balance. They are frightened and thrown into confusion by the cries of the middle class of society. We see this middle class trying to persuade kings that their rights are confined to sitting on the throne, while the people are to govern. They attack all that past centuries have left us that is holy and worthy of man's respect. They deny the value of the past. They declare themselves the masters of the future.

There is a rule of conduct established by the experience of centuries, as well as by everyday life. This rule declares that one must not dream of reforms while moved by emotion. Wisdom directs that at such moments we should limit ourselves to keeping things as they are.

Let the monarchs strongly adopt the principle of stability [remaining firm or fixed]. This will not prevent the development of what is good. But it is for those who are burdened with the heavy task of government, not for middle-class reformers to look out for the well-being of their people.

The first and greatest concern of the large majority of every nation is the stability of the laws—never their change. Therefore, let the governments govern. Let them keep their institutions [established laws and practices], both ancient and modern. It is at all times dangerous to touch them. It certainly would not be wise to do so now, in the general confusion.

Let the governments not allow experience to lose all its rights in order to make way for dangerous experiments. Let the governments not seek to win over those parties who aim to destroy their power by giving in to them. To give in will not win over these people. It will only encourage them in trying to seize power.

Let the great monarchs also strengthen their union [the four-power alliance]. Let them prove to the world that it ensures the peace of Europe. It is powerful only to maintain calm at a time when so many attacks are directed against it. The principle of kings is protective. They threaten only those who disturb public order.

Prince Clemens von Metternich, chancellor of the Austrian Empire. He once described himself as "a rock of order." What do you think he meant by this phrase?

Adapted from Prince Richard Metternich (ed.), *Memoirs of Prince Metternich* (Vol. 3).

▶ **THINKING IT THROUGH**

1. What arguments does Metternich give against making changes?
2. Under what conditions does he admit that changes might be made?
3. "Metternich was trying to turn the clock of Europe back to 1789."
   a. Do you agree with this statement? Why or why not?
   b. Would you expect him to succeed? Why or why not?
4. Do you think the four-power alliance was a good way to keep the peace? Why or why not?

9. HOW DID REVOLUTIONS DESTROY THE METTERNICH SYSTEM?

Metternich's efforts to "turn back the clock" were only partly successful. After tasting freedom, the common people of Europe would no longer accept the absolute rule of the Old Regime. The result was wave after wave of revolutions. Examine the following chart. Notice that revolutions struck every part of Europe except Great Britain and Russia. Why do you think these two countries escaped?

Waves of Revolutions, 1815–1848

Date	Country	Cause	Outcome
Before 1820	Spain's colonies in Central and South America	To gain independence from Spain.	Succeeded, largely because of the protection of Great Britain and the United States.
1820	Spain	To overthrow the reactionary king Ferdinand VII, who was sending troops to reconquer Latin America.	Crushed by a French army acting for the four-power alliance.
	Kingdom of the Two Sicilies (in southern Italy)	To overthrow a reactionary ruler.	Crushed by Austria, which was acting for the four-power alliance.
1823–1829	Greece	To gain independence from the Turkish Empire.	Succeeded because of help from Russia, Great Britain, and France.
1830	France	To overthrow the reactionary Charles X, brother of Louis XVI and XVIII.	Established a limited monarchy under Louis Philippe, cousin of Charles X.
	Belgium	To gain independence from Holland.	Succeeded because of the support of Great Britain and France.
	Poland	To gain independence from Russia.	Crushed by the Russian army.

	Some states of Italy and Germany	To overthrow reactionary rulers and to gain reforms.	Crushed by local authorities with help from Austria and Prussia.
1848	France	To overthrow Louis Philippe, who ruled for the rich.	Established France's Second Republic.
	Austria	To win reforms.	Metternich fled. Emperor Ferdinand I left his throne. The new emperor, Francis Joseph, promised reforms.
	Hungary, Bohemia	To win independence from Austria.	Crushed with Russian help.
	Prussia	To gain reforms.	A few reforms were made, including the election of a Diet (legislature)
	Germany	To unite the country.	Failed after King Frederick William IV of Prussia refused to accept the crown of a united Germany.
	Italy	To overthrow reactionary rulers and to drive out the Austrians who supported them.	Crushed by Austria.

▶ INTERPRETING THE CHART

1. The four-power alliance failed to crush the revolutions in the Spanish colonies and in Greece.
   a. Why did it fail in these cases?
   b. What weakness of the Metternich system did these failures reveal?
2. "When France sneezes, Europe catches cold." Explain this statement, using evidence from the chart.
3. Analyze the nineteenth-century revolutions by classifying them according to the following categories:
   a. liberal revolution. (This type sought constitutional reforms and a more representative government.)
   b. nationalist revolution. (This type sought to unite a nation or to win independence from foreign rule.)
   c. revolution for both liberal and nationalist causes.
4. Which do you think proved stronger in the end—the ideas of the French Revolution or Metternich's system of reaction? Support your answer.

Reviewing Chapter 3

1. Why was Napoleon Bonaparte able to seize power in France?
2. What improvements did Napoleon make in his country?
3. Why did conditions in France and the conquered countries grow worse in the later years of Napoleon's rule?
4. Why was Napoleon finally defeated and overthrown?
5. Explain how the ideas of the French Revolution were spread throughout Western Europe—first by Napoleon, then by the revolutions against the Metternich system.
6. What types of revolutions struck Europe between 1815 and 1848?
7. In what important ways was Europe a very different place in 1848 than in 1789?

1. Bonaparte promised the French people "order, liberty, security, and prosperity."
   a. Why did these promises appeal to the French people in 1799?
   b. Could he possibly keep all four promises? Why or why not?
   c. Does a political leader usually keep all his promises after he gains power? Explain, using examples to support your argument.
2. The French people loved Napoleon much more than the kings who preceded him.
   a. Why was this true?
   b. Do you think a military hero like Napoleon could gain and hold power in a large modern nation today? Why or why not?
3. England's policy for centuries was to maintain a balance of power in Europe. This means that if any one European nation threatened to become too powerful, England would form or support an alliance of several other nations against the rising nation.
   a. Why did England follow this policy against both Louis XIV and Napoleon?
   b. Do you think it was a wise policy? Why or why not?
4. The European powers crushed the revolutions of 1820 in Spain and Italy, but allowed the Greeks to win their freedom.
   a. Why did they take such opposing stands? (See the maps on page 94.)
   b. Was Metternich right or wrong in urging the powers to crush every revolution, regardless of the circumstances? Explain.
5. Nationalism was already a powerful force in Europe in the early nineteenth century.
   a. What role did nationalism play in Napoleon's early victories?
   b. How did it contribute to his later defeats?
   c. How did it affect Metternich's system for keeping peace in Europe?
   d. Is it still a powerful force in the world today? Support your answer.
6. "Fight any change. Do not think. Obey the emperor and the Church."
   a. Is the above comment by Metternich typical of his political views? Explain.
   b. Many people in eighteenth-century Europe held similar views. Why are such ideas considered reactionary today?
   c. Could any modern government impose such views on its people? Why or why not?

ROLE-PLAYING: THE INQUIRING REPORTER

Was Napoleon a Great Leader or a Tyrant?

Be prepared to take a role in an activity in which an "inquiring reporter" asks several people of the early nineteenth century what they think of Napoleon as a leader. These should include Frenchmen and other Europeans—notably Englishmen, Germans, Spaniards, and Russians. The inquiring reporter should begin his interview of each person with the question above.

The interviews should take place at three successive times, according to the following scenes:

Scene 1. In 1800, soon after Napoleon gained control of the French government.

Scene 2. In 1809, when Napoleon was at the height of his power.

Scene 3. In 1815, after Napoleon was defeated at Waterloo and sent to St. Helena.

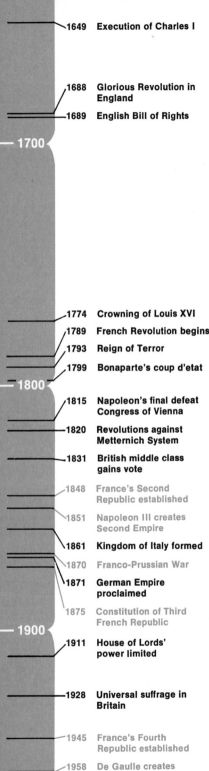

CHAPTER 4

How Did France Become a Democracy?

The many changes of government in France between 1789 and 1848 were discussed in Chapters 2 and 3. In this chapter you will read how France, after two more changes, established a parliamentary government similar to the British. Basic changes in the government have continued. Today France has a presidential system, more like the American government than the British. Why have the French had so many changes of government? What have been the results? These are questions to keep in mind as you read this chapter.

60

1. HOW WAS A SECOND REPUBLIC ESTABLISHED IN FRANCE?

To understand more fully the many changes of government in France, it is necessary to examine the conflicts between the different classes of French society. The Revolution of 1789 was, for the most part, the work of the middle class. The city workers became unhappy with middle class rule. They seized power for a time under France's First Republic. This was the period of radical reforms, accompanied by the Reign of Terror. These actions aroused such great opposition that the middle class regained power. It held its position until the rise of Napoleon Bonaparte.

Napoleon tried to heal the wounds left by the Revolution. He worked to win the support of all classes, including even the nobility and the clergy. He appealed to nationalism, to winning glory for France. This united all classes.

Louis XVIII came to the throne after Napoleon's downfall. He was supported mainly by the upper classes. He wisely allowed the middle class a voice in his government. Louis was succeeded by his brother, Charles X. The new king tried to take away the rights of the middle class. Charles was overthrown in 1830. His cousin Louis Philippe was put on the throne. Louis Philippe gained his strength mainly from the upper middle class of wealthy industrialists, merchants, and bankers. His rule is known in French history as the Bourgeois (middle class) Monarchy.

a. The Revolution of February 1848

Many businessmen grew rich under Louis Philippe. The workers, however, became more and more dissatisfied. They led the revolution that overthrew the king in February 1848. The reading that follows is by Alexis de Tocqueville, a famous political writer. He is telling what happened after the fall of the monarchy.

Louis Philippe being sworn in as king of France. The audience is made up of the wealthy businessmen who supported him. What kind of policy do you think this backing committed him to?

Revolutionaries celebrating the creation of the French Republic in 1848. The revolution was led by the workers. What do you think they expected the new republic to do for them?

I spent the whole afternoon walking about Paris. What struck me was the popular character of the revolution that had just taken place. It had given power to the people—that is to say, to the classes who work with their hands. The lower orders had suddenly become masters of Paris.

Throughout this day, I did not see in Paris a single one of the former agents of the public authority. There was not a soldier, not a policeman. The National Guard had disappeared. The people alone bore arms. They guarded the public buildings, watched, gave orders, and punished. It was an unusual thing to see the people who had owned nothing of all this large city now so loaded with riches.

The fright of all the other classes was extreme. Since nothing like this had ever been seen before, many people expected acts of violence. But I knew the people of Paris too well. I knew that their first movements in times of revolution are generous. Besides, we French have spent many years in uprisings. There has grown up among us a kind of moral code for times of disorder. According to this unwritten rule, murder is tolerated, but theft is forbidden. What reassured me still more was that the workers' feelings had not had time to take fire. The government had fallen undefended by others or even by itself.

Soon a thousand strange plans for reform were put forth. Everyone came forward with a plan. This one printed his plan in the papers. That one displayed his plan on the posters with which the walls were soon covered. A third shouted his design loud-mouthed in the open air. One aimed at destroying the inequality of wealth. Another tried to end the inequality of education. A third undertook to do away with the oldest of all inequalities, that between man and woman.

Adapted from Alexis de Tocqueville, *Recollections* (translated by Alexander de Mattos), The Macmillan Company, 1896, pp. 92–101.

▶ THINKING IT THROUGH

1. In what ways was the revolution of 1848 different from previous revolutions in France?
2. Many plans for reform were prepared during the revolution.
   a. Why do you think so many reform plans were put forth at this time?
   b. Were these plans practical? Why or why not?

b. "The Terrible June Days" of 1848

The revolution upset business, and many people were thrown out of work. The workers' leaders discussed many plans, including a Socialist one, for dealing with these economic problems. Meanwhile, the leaders of the middle class quietly gained control of the new government. At first, they tried to calm the workers by establishing "National Workshops," in which the government provided work for the unemployed. This program proved very expensive, however. So it was gradually cut back.

Finally, the workers took to the streets again. Their battle cry was "Bread or Lead." The outcome of this second struggle is described below by Karl Marx, "the father of modern socialism." As you read, notice how Marx explains the role of the workers. Do you agree with his viewpoint?

The February Revolution was won by the workers. . . . The proletarians [workers] regarded themselves, and rightly, as the victors of February, and made the proud claims of victors. They had to be vanquished [defeated] on the streets, they had to be shown that they were worsted [beaten] as soon as they fought not *with* the bourgeoisie, but *against* the bourgeoisie. . . . But the real point of attack was, as we have seen, the *National Ateliers* [National Workshops]. . . . The Executive Commission [government] began by making entry into the *National Ateliers* more difficult and by banishing workers not born in Paris to Cologne, ostensibly [supposedly] for the construction of earthworks [fortifications made of earth]. Finally, on June 21, a decree appeared in the *Moniteur* [an official newspaper] which ordered the forcible expulsion of all unmarried workers from the *National Ateliers,* or their enrollment in the army.

The workers were left with no choice; they had to starve or fight. They answered on June 22 with the tremendous insurrection [uprising] in which the first great battle was fought between the two classes that split modern society. It was a fight for the preservation or annihilation of the *bourgeois order.* . . .

It is well-known how the workers, . . . without chiefs, without a common plan, . . . lacking weapons, held in check for five days the army, . . . the Parisian National Guard, and the National Guard that streamed in from the provinces. It is well-known how the bourgeoisie compensated itself for the mortal anguish [suffering] it underwent by unheard-of brutality, and massacred over 3,000 prisoners.

Reprinted from Karl Marx, *The Class Struggles in France* (International Publishers Company, Inc.), 1935, p. 57.

▶ **THINKING IT THROUGH**

1. In the above description does Marx take the side of the workers or the bourgeoisie? Quote from the article to support your answer.
2. Do you agree or disagree with Marx on the following observations?
   a. The fighting was the fault of the bourgeoisie.
   b. The French middle class would have been destroyed if it had lost.
   Explain each answer.
3. Why is this incident known in French history as "the Terrible June Days"?

2. *HOW WAS FRANCE'S SECOND EMPIRE ESTABLISHED?*

Louis Napoleon, who was elected president of France in 1848. He was the nephew of Napoleon Bonaparte. How might this have helped him win the election?

The Second Republic lasted only three years. Its fall was a result of the bitter class conflicts of 1848. An election for president was held later in the year. One candidate was put up by the workers. A second candidate was the general who had crushed their revolt. Most Frenchmen did not support either one. They voted, instead, for Louis Napoleon Bonaparte, a nephew of Napoleon I. To avoid arrest, Louis Napoleon had spent many years in England, the United States, and other foreign lands. He had professed democratic, and even Socialistic ideas.

a. The Presidential Election of 1848

The selection below contains the promises Louis Napoleon made in 1848, when he was running for president. Would you expect him to keep these promises?

In order to call me from exile, you have elected me a representative of the people. Just when you are choosing a president for the republic, my name presents itself to you as a symbol of order and safety. The memory of the emperor [Napoleon I] protects me and inspires your votes.

I am not moved by dreams of the empire and war. I was brought up in free countries. I shall ever remain faithful to the duties that your votes and the will of the assembly impose on me.

If elected president, I shall shrink from no danger, from no sacrifice, to defend society. I shall devote myself wholly to the strengthening of the republic. My greatest honor will be to hand, after four years of office, to my successor the public power strengthened, its liberties untouched, and a genuine progress accomplished.

Adapted from C. E. de Maupas, *The Story of the Coup d'Etat.*

▶ **THINKING IT THROUGH**

1. Why has it been said that in 1848 the French people "voted for a name"?
2. The above speech shows the kind of campaign Louis Napoleon conducted.
   a. How did he appeal for the votes of the French people?
   b. Do you think his promises won him many votes? Explain.
3. If you had been a French voter in that election, would you have voted for Louis Napoleon? Why or why not?

b. The Program of Napoleon III

Less than four years after he became president, Louis Napoleon Bonaparte staged a coup d'etat. Then he had himself crowned as Emperor NAPOLEON III. *(The son of Napoleon I, who died young, was considered Napoleon II.) In the speech that follows, the new emperor tells the French people how he intends to rule them. Would you have believed his promises this time?*

There is a fear among the people which I must deny. In a spirit of distrust, certain persons declare the empire means war. But I say the empire means peace.

It means peace because France desires it. When France is satisfied, the world is calm.

I admit, however, that I, like the emperor [Napoleon I], have indeed conquests to make. I wish, like him, to conquer the hostile parties within France. They are now ruining themselves without profit to anybody.

I wish to conquer for religion, morality, and comfortable living a large part of the population [the working class]. In the midst of a country of faith and belief, these people scarcely

Louis Napoleon, known as Emperor Napoleon III, is shown here speaking to his legislative assembly. He allowed the assembly practically no power. Why do you think he did this instead of dissolving it entirely?

know the teachings of Christ. In the midst of the most fertile land in the world, they can scarcely enjoy the most necessary products.

We have large uncultivated territories to clear and routes to open. There are harbors to deepen and rivers to open to ships. There are canals to finish and railroads to complete. We have opposite the city of Marseilles a large kingdom [Algeria in North Africa] to absorb. We have to connect our great western ports with the American continent by those rapid means of transportation which we still lack.

That is how I understand the empire. Such are the conquests that I think about. All of you around me who wish, like myself, the welfare of our fatherland, you are my soldiers.

Adapted from F. M. Anderson, *Constitutions and Other Select Documents Illustrative of the History of France*, pp. 539–540, 558–560.

▶ THINKING IT THROUGH

1. "Louis Napoleon Bonaparte followed in the footsteps of his famous uncle." Do you agree with this statement? Why or why not?
2. Why did Napoleon III stress that he stood for peace?

3. As this speech indicates, Louis Napoleon made a broad appeal among the people of France.
   a. How did he appeal to religious Catholics? The workers? The middle class? All patriotic Frenchmen?
   b. Would you have trusted his promises? Why or why not?
4. Napoleon III asked the French people to vote on whether they supported his new government. A large majority voted "Yes." Why do you think they did so?
5. "The Second Empire was a result of the class conflicts in the Second Republic." Do you agree? Why or why not?

3. WAS THE THIRD FRENCH REPUBLIC DEMOCRATIC?

Despite his promises, Napoleon III engaged in three wars in Europe and three wars to conquer colonies overseas. His Second Empire came to an end in 1870, when the Prussians defeated his armies and took him prisoner. For the third time, France became a republic.

For a few years, the THIRD REPUBLIC was in danger. This was because the various classes of society once again struggled for power. Then the middle class gained control and established a parliamentary government. This government lasted until Hitler conquered France in 1940. Thus the Third Republic was by far the longest-lasting French government since the overthrow of Louis XVI in 1789.

In this scene, French troops vainly try to keep the Prussian army out of Paris. Even though many Frenchmen disliked Napoleon III's government, they fought hard against the Prussian attack. Why do you think they did so?

a. The Machinery of the French Government

The following diagram shows the government of France's Third Republic. This government was based on the British parliamentary system. Turn to the diagram of the British government on page 20. Compare the two diagrams, noting the resemblances and the differences. Then answer the questions that follow this diagram.

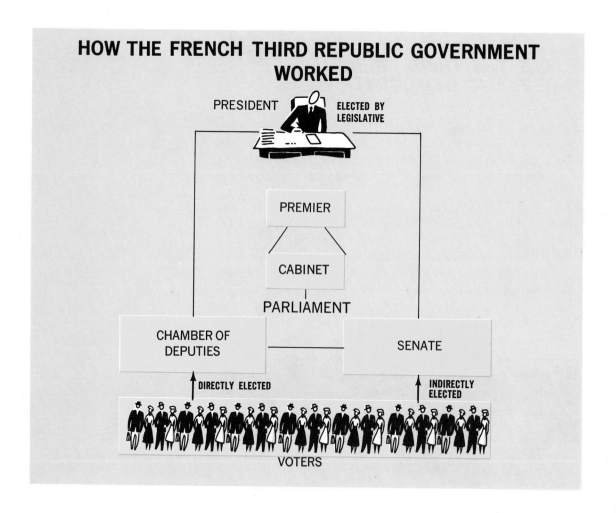

HOW THE FRENCH THIRD REPUBLIC GOVERNMENT WORKED

PRESIDENT — ELECTED BY LEGISLATIVE

PREMIER

CABINET

PARLIAMENT

CHAMBER OF DEPUTIES — SENATE

↑ DIRECTLY ELECTED ↑ INDIRECTLY ELECTED

VOTERS

▶ INTERPRETING THE DIAGRAM

1. The most important parts of the British government are the monarchy, the prime minister and cabinet, the House of Commons, and the House of Lords.
   a. Compare this system with the French by deciding whether France has any body similar to each of the British.

  b. In what ways does the French government appear to be modeled on the British?

2. What important differences do you find in the two systems?

b. An Unstable Government

France enjoyed a long period of peace and economic progress from 1870 until 1914, when the First World War broke out. The period between the first and second world wars, however, was a troubled one. During both periods, the government of the Third Republic was very unstable. On the average, a PREMIER *(prime minister) and his cabinet held office only about six months. Some lasted only a few months, a few weeks, or even a few hours!*

Many aspects of the French government were based on the British model. Why, then, was the French form so unstable? The main reason was the difference in the number of political parties. Great Britain, like the United States, has only two major political parties. Elections are, to a large extent, contests to decide which party will control the government. In France and a few other democratic countries, there are many political parties. Each party usually represents the views of a certain class or group in the society.

In a many-party system, it rarely happens that a single party has a majority of the seats in the legislature. Instead, the premier gets the majority he needs by forming a COALITION *(alliance) of several parties. If a single party leaves the premier's coalition, he often loses his majority and has to resign. The many-party system is the basic reason why the government of France's Third Republic was unstable.*

The diagram that follows reveals this situation more clearly. It shows the political parties in the Chamber of Deputies after the election of 1936. Which party's leader became premier at that time?

Note the following unusual features of the French government in the 1930's. Then answer the questions below the diagram.

1. The Communists and the Socialists both wanted to overthrow the middle-class government and establish a Socialist state. Yet the two leftist parties were usually bitter rivals. They managed to work together only in the late 1930's. At that time, they were frightened by the rise of Hitler in Germany.

2. The Dissident Communists (those who "disagree") and the Dissident Socialists held similar views as the regular Communists and Socialists. Unlike the regular members, however, they did not belong to the official parties. Instead, each deputy decided for himself how he would vote on any issue.

3. The Radical Socialists and Left Radicals, despite their names, were middle-class parties. They favored only a few mild reforms.

4. The Democratic Alliance and the Union of Democratic Republicans each consisted of several parties. Their members, like the Dissident Communists and Dissident Socialists, voted as they wished.

FRENCH ELECTION OF 1936
DISTRIBUTION OF SEATS IN THE CHAMBER OF DEPUTIES

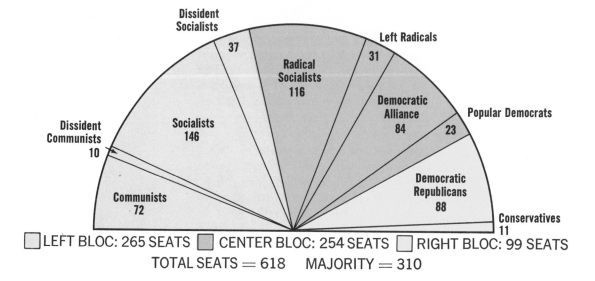

Dissident Socialists **37**

Left Radicals **31**

Radical Socialists **116**

Democratic Alliance **84**

Popular Democrats

Dissident Communists **10**

Socialists **146**

23

Democratic Republicans **88**

Communists **72**

Conservatives **11**

LEFT BLOC: 265 SEATS CENTER BLOC: 254 SEATS RIGHT BLOC: 99 SEATS

TOTAL SEATS = 618   MAJORITY = 310

▶ INTERPRETING THE DIAGRAM

1. Judging by the diagram, why would it be difficult for the leader of any party to gain a majority of the votes in the Chamber?
2. In the election of 1936, which parties were members of the left bloc? Which were members of the center bloc? Which were members of the right bloc?
3. Between 1936 and 1940, when the Third Republic was ended, the premier was usually the leader of either the Socialist or the Radical Socialist Party.
   a. Why was this true?
   b. Why did his government usually last only a short while?
4. Suggest some changes that might have made the French government more stable.

4. HOW DID GENERAL DE GAULLE ESTABLISH THE FIFTH REPUBLIC?

Early in World War II, France surrendered to the invading German army. Hitler set up a French government (known as the Vichy government) that worked with and for the Germans. When

Hitler was defeated, this government quickly fell and the Fourth Republic was established. The new government proved as weak and unstable as the Third Republic had been. Class conflicts continued in the country. A new source of trouble was a strong independence movement in France's colonies. Wars for independence broke out in two valuable colonies, Indo-China and Algeria. These wars lasted for years. France finally had to withdraw from both colonies.

a. The President's Position

For a time, divisions over the war in Algeria threatened to set off a civil war in France. The government of the Fourth Republic was unable to deal with the situation. Government leaders called to power a hero of World War II, General CHARLES DE GAULLE. *The selection below tells how de Gaulle established the* FIFTH REPUBLIC *of France. He changed the French government from a parliamentary system to a presidential system. The French government now resembles that of the United States, rather than the British government.*

De Gaulle had the final say in drawing up the new constitution of the Fifth Republic. The constitution followed his ideas of a presidential republic with a strong executive. Control of the army, foreign relations, and relations with the French colonies was reserved for the president. He also had the right to dismiss the National Assembly. Thus the president of the French Republic was raised from a mere symbol to a position of great power. He has more power than the president of the United States, who cannot send Congress home.

The new constitution was published on July 29, 1958. The referendum [the people's vote on whether they favored the new government] was set for September 28. On September 4, de Gaulle made the following appeal to the people of France:

"What is of the greatest importance to the government from now on is its effectiveness and stability. We live in a time when great forces are changing the world. We must develop rapidly in the scientific, economic, and social areas. Thus it is for us, for the people we are, for the century and the world in which we live, that the new constitution has been created. Under it the country will be efficiently led by those whom it chooses and to whom it gives its trust.

This, Frenchmen and Frenchwomen, is what inspires the

General Charles de Gaulle, the World War II hero whom the French people later elected president of their country. Would you expect a military man to make a good president? Why or why not?

De Gaulle making a speech while president of France. He wanted to be a strong president, for he felt this would make the government more stable. Do you agree with his reasoning? Why or why not?

constitution that will be given to you for your approval on September 28. With all my heart, I ask you in the name of France to vote 'Yes.'

If you do not approve it, we will return to the troubled days you have known. If you do, the republic will be strong and effective. Approving the constitution will be a positive declaration of the national will. It will show that our country has recovered its unity and has regained its chance for greatness.

Vive la Republique!
Vive la France!"

The great day came and more French people voted than ever before in history. Nearly 85 percent of eligible voters went to the polls. When the votes were counted, 79.5 percent were for the new constitution—or, rather, for de Gaulle.

As soon as the constitution was approved, a general election was called to elect the new National Assembly. A great many people wanted to hop on the de Gaulle bandwagon. A new party was formed, the Union for the New Republic (U.N.R.), which advertised itself as "the Gaullist Party."

Adapted from *The de Gaulle Nobody Knows* by Alden Hatch. Copyright © 1960 by Alden Hatch. By permission of Hawthorn Books, Inc.

▶ THINKING IT THROUGH

1. Compare the parliamentary system and the presidential one, by answering the following questions:
   a. What is the major difference between the two systems?
   b. Why did de Gaulle prefer the presidential system?
   c. Why were many Frenchmen afraid of a strong president?
2. In his speech de Gaulle gives the French people reasons for supporting his new constitution.
   a. What reasons does he give them?
   b. How does he appeal to their feelings of nationalism?

3. If you had been a French voter in 1958, would you have voted for de Gaulle's constitution? Why or why not?
4. Do you approve of the new Gaullist party that developed? Why or why not?

b. The Downfall of de Gaulle

Many people wondered whether de Gaulle would try to make himself the sole ruler of France, as Napoleon I and Napoleon III had done. Others thought that he and his Fifth Republic would be overthrown by still another revolution. Actually, de Gaulle remained president for ten years. He began by making the reforms that France needed. He also worked hard to make France an important power, despite the fact that it was no longer a large and powerful nation. He finally retired from office when the French people voted against him on an unimportant question of local government. The Fifth Republic continued under a new president. The following passage expresses one view of the passing of the de Gaulle era.

During the ten years, ten months, and twenty-eight days of his reign, de Gaulle had become the spirit of France. Despite failing eyesight and old age, he had overcome a series of crises and conspiracies that would have felled any less a leader. He survived some half a dozen attempts upon his life. Only last spring, French students set off a wave of riots and strikes that almost toppled his regime. De Gaulle once again surprised the world. At the climax of the disorders, the entire French nation lay paralyzed on the brink of disaster. The proud old general delivered a bold four-minute television address. It signaled the end of this "May revolution." In the parliamentary elections that followed, the Gaullists won the most lopsided [largest] majority of any party in French history.

Yet now, almost in the twinkling of an eye, de Gaulle was gone. The news of his defeat at the polls and his resignation from office spread around the world. The question then rose, How on earth had it happened?

That was a question that historians would probably argue for decades to come. In the meantime, it seemed safe to say that the French had grown increasingly weary of de Gaulle's one-man rule. They were no longer sure that his departure from office would automatically be followed by the deluge [flood].

▶ THINKING IT THROUGH

1. Why did the French people give de Gaulle strong support at first?
2. Why did they give de Gaulle's party a huge majority after the disorders of May 1969?
3. Why did they vote against de Gaulle only a few months later?
4. Do you think de Gaulle's ten-year "rule" was good for France? Explain.
5. Do you expect the Fifth Republic to last for a long time? Why or why not?

5. *WHAT DIFFERENT FORMS OF GOVERNMENT HAS FRANCE HAD?*

You have read in Chapters 2–4 that France has seen many different forms of government since the eighteenth century. The most important of these are shown on the time line that follows. Study the time line; then answer the questions below it. If you need additional information, refer back to the appropriate reading.

THE CHANGING FORMS OF THE FRENCH GOVERNMENT

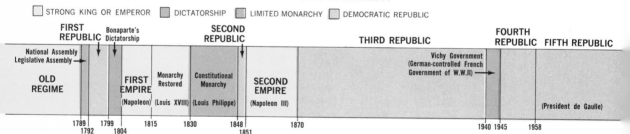

☐ STRONG KING OR EMPEROR ◼ DICTATORSHIP ▨ LIMITED MONARCHY ☐ DEMOCRATIC REPUBLIC

▶ INTERPRETING THE TIME LINE

1. What four different types of government has France had? Give one or two examples of each type.
2. Which government ruled for the longest time since 1789?
3. Which government is associated with Charles de Gaulle?
4. "France gained democracy by revolution, not by evolution." Do you agree with this statement? Why or why not?

Reviewing Chapter 4

SUMMING UP

1. Why has France had a large number of revolutions and other changes of government since 1789?

2. Today the French people still have differing attitudes about the kind of government they want.
   a. Why might many Frenchmen want a strong government?
   b. Why might many others be against a strong government?
   c. Has the Fifth Republic been satisfying both those who want a strong government and those who do not? Explain.

3. Which of the French governments described in Chapters 2–4 do you consider the most successful? Why?

FOR FURTHER INQUIRY

1. Napoleon III was often referred to as "Napoleon the Little."
   a. Why was he given this title?
   b. Do you think it was an accurate description? Why or why not?

2. When running for office, Louis Napoleon promised not to engage in foreign conquests once he gained power.
   a. Why did he break his promise?
   b. Was he wise to do so? Explain.

3. France had a weak executive under the Third and Fourth Republics. It now has a strong executive under the Fifth Republic. Which is more effective? Why? (Use the experiences of France, Great Britain, and the United States to support your answer.)

4. The French people are still politically split into a number of different factions (groups with different ideas).
   a. Why did these splits develop?
   b. Are they desirable or undesirable? Why?
   c. Does the United States face the problem of disunity today? Support your answer.
   d. What can a government do to unify its people?

5. France and several other democratic nations have a number of political parties.
   a. What are the strengths of the multiparty system? The two-party system?
   b. What are the weaknesses of each of these systems?

ROLE-PLAYING: DEBATE

Resolved: The Presidential Form of Democratic Government Is Better Than the Parliamentary System

Two teams should debate the merits of the presidential and the parliamentary forms of democracy, one team defending the above statement and the other opposing it. Be prepared to join either team. In the debate each team should use the experiences of France, Great Britain, and the United States to support its side of the issue. The class should ask questions of both teams, and weigh the evidence presented.

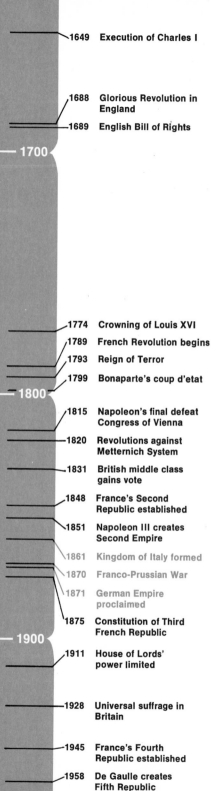

CHAPTER **5**

How Did the Spirit of Nationalism Change Europe?

Representative democracy is an important form of government. It began in Western Europe and spread to the rest of the world. A second important political development also was born in the West. This was the rise of nations and of NATION-ALISM (a feeling of deep loyalty to one's nation). Chapters 2 and 3 explored the tremendous effects of nationalism during the French Revolution. Its spirit inspired France's citizen armies to drive back the foreigners invading their country.

76

Napoleon, without meaning to do so, awakened nationalism in the rest of Europe. First he stirred up the peoples of the different countries by bringing them the reforms of the Revolution. Then he imposed heavy taxes on them, and in other ways tried to bring them more firmly under his control. He also took their young men for his armies. These people rose against him and brought about his downfall.

Metternich also unintentionally strengthened the spirit of nationalism. Europe had many nationalities—that is, groups of people with the same language, religion, and customs. Metternich tried to keep various SUBJECT NATIONALITIES (peoples under foreign control) from setting up their own nations. This was a major reason for the revolutions that swept Europe in 1820, 1830, and 1848. Most of these revolutions, as you have seen, ended in failure.

The Industrial Revolution was still another factor in the rise of nationalism. Improvements in transportation and communication brought people in different parts of a country closer together. Schools, newspapers, and books taught them to think of themselves as one people and to want independence.

In this chapter, you will see how the forces of nationalism reshaped Europe during the late nineteenth and early twentieth centuries. Two new nations—the Kingdom of Italy and the German Empire—were formed. Three existing empires —the Austrian Empire, the Ottoman (Turkish) Empire, and the Russian Empire—were broken up. As you read, notice how the spirit of nationalism led to these changes.

Workers and peasants battle government troops in this scene from the revolution in Vienna in 1848. What problems do you think street fighting posed the revolutionaries? What advantages did it afford them?

1. HOW DID MAZZINI ORGANIZE "YOUNG ITALY"?

Italy was still a "geographic expression" at the beginning of the nineteenth century. Surrounded by seas and mountains, it formed a natural unit. Yet it was not a united nation. Instead, it was divided into a dozen or so small states. (See the map on page 83.)

The nationalist feelings of the Italian people were first aroused by Napoleon. They welcomed him both as their liberator from the Old Regime and as a fellow Italian. (He was born on the island of Corsica, which had long been a part of Italy. It had become a part of France only a short time before Napoleon was born.) Napoleon also reduced the number of different countries in Italy.

The Congress of Vienna disregarded the feelings of the Italian people. It undid Napoleon's changes and cut up Italy again into a number of small states. Austria took over a large part of northern Italy. Austrian troops helped to crush the Italian revolutions of 1820, 1830, and 1848.

GIUSEPPE MAZZINI was a leader of the struggle to drive out the Austrians and unify Italy. To do so, he formed a secret organization named "Young Italy." The following reading is the oath its members took. Does this oath reveal why Mazzini was called "the soul of Italian unification"?

Giuseppe Mazzini, the Italian revolutionary whose writings spread the dream of a unified Italy. In what other ways can a writer be important to a revolution?

In the name of God and of Italy;

In the name of all the martyrs of the holy Italian cause who have been killed by foreign and Italian tyrants;

By the duties that bind me to the land in which God has placed me, and to the brothers whom God has given me;

By the love I bear to the country that gave my mother birth, and will be the home of my children;

By the hatred I bear to evil, injustice, and despotic [absolute] rule;

By the blush that rises to my brow when I stand before the citizens of other lands, to know that I have no rights of citizenship, no country, and no national flag;

By the memory of our former greatness, and the sense of our present low condition;

By the tears of Italian mothers for their sons dead on the scaffold, in prison, or in exile;

By the suffering of the millions—

I, _____, believe in the mission given by God to Italy, and in the duty of every Italian to try to fulfill it. I am sure that where God has decided that a nation shall be, He has given the power to create it. The people are the holders of that power. In the people lies the secret of victory.

I give my name to Young Italy, an association of men having the same faith, and swear:

To devote myself wholly and forever to make Italy one free, independent, republican nation;

To promote by every means in my power—whether by written or spoken word, or by action—the education of my Italian brothers towards the aim of Young Italy;

To obey all instructions given me by those who represent with me the union of my Italian brothers;

To keep the secret of these instructions, even at the cost of my life;

To assist my brothers of the association both by action and counsel—

NOW AND FOREVER.

This do I swear. I call down on my head the anger of God, the hatred of man, and the disgrace of a perjurer [liar], if I ever betray the whole or a part of this oath.

Adapted from *Joseph Mazzini: His Life, Writings, and Political Principles,* pp. 72–74.

▶ THINKING IT THROUGH

1. Compare Italy today and in the early nineteenth century by answering the following questions:
   a. Why was Italy called a "geographic expression" in the early nineteenth century?
   b. Why is it now considered a "geographic unit" instead?
2. In the oath, Mazzini makes appeals to Italian nationalism.
   a. What are some of these appeals?
   b. Which of them do you consider the most powerful? Why?
3. In the oath Mazzini speaks of "the memory of our former greatness" and "our present low condition."
   a. What does he mean by each of these comments?
   b. What does he ask the members of Young Italy to do?
4. Mazzini gained a following especially among *young* Italians.
   a. Why was this true?
   b. If you had been a young Italian of that time, would you have joined him? Why or why not?

2. HOW DID ITALY BECOME A NATION?

Mazzini started several revolts, but only the one in 1848 was even partly successful. The man who actually began to unify Italy was Count CAMILLO DI CAVOUR, "the brain of Italian unification." Cavour was prime minister of the Kingdom of Sardinia in northern Italy. He made a number of reforms in that kingdom. Many Italians began to look to Sardinia for leadership. Cavour also formed an alliance with France and provoked Austria into attacking Sardinia. Together, the French and Sardinians defeated Austria. Sardinia took over part of Austria's holdings in northern Italy. The other states of northern Italy then joined with Sardinia.

However, the Pope's holdings in central Italy and the Kingdom of the Two Sicilies in the south still remained separate countries. The liberation of southern Italy and Sicily was the work of a member of Young Italy, GIUSEPPE GARIBALDI. With a small force known as "the Thousand Red Shirts," Garibaldi defeated the much larger forces of the ruler of southern Italy. Read the following description of a battle scene. Then figure out how Garibaldi accomplished this military miracle.

The most brilliant moment in the action on October 1 was the recapture of the battery of artillery at the foot of Mont St. Angelo. Garibaldi arrived at nine o'clock. The enemy was

Camillo di Cavour, the Italian political leader who forged the Kingdom of Italy. He once said that if politicians did for themselves what they do in the service of their country, they would be considered "rascals and rogues." What do you think he meant by this remark?

Giuseppe Garibaldi and his army of Red Shirts preparing to sail for Italy to fight the Austrians. Compare this scene with the revolution in Vienna on page 77. In what ways do Garibaldi's forces seem better prepared for battle than the Viennese?

then attacking this battery with all his strength because it was causing him severe loss. The triple [three-section] battery courageously resisted the attack. It never slowed its fire. Suddenly the battery at the foot of the hill became silent. Some 2,500 royalist soldiers had rushed upon the guns, spiked five of them, and killed several of the men.

Garibaldi soon noticed the silence of his favorily battery. This disaster would probably have lost him the battle. He started off at once, followed by his staff. Collecting what men he could, he cried out in a voice that caused all to shudder, "We are going to die. But the Italians must win the day. At all other points, we have conquered." Followed by 100 men, Garibaldi went forward at a fast pace.

Suddenly some enemy troops appeared. Garibaldi went up to them, shouting, "Long live Italy!" Some of his men came up at the same time and the enemy fled. Garibaldi was wounded slightly in the stomach. His trousers were torn by two or three bullets. "If I only had another pair," he said.

Without further words, he continued his march toward a battalion of 150 Hungarians, who were a part of his army. Pointing to the enemy, who still held his battery, he cried out to the Hungarians, "Forward, my lads; get rid of them for me!" The Hungarians, without waiting to count the numbers of the enemy, rushed forward. After a contest of twenty minutes, the battery was retaken. Once more, it poured its storm of grapeshot [small cannon balls] on the enemy troops. They fled in confusion across the fields. The day was now won.

Adapted from Theodore Dwight, *The Life of General Garibaldi*, pp. 414–415.

▶ THINKING IT THROUGH

1. What reasons for Garibaldi's success are shown in this description?
2. Garibaldi shouted "Long live Italy" at the enemy troops.
   a. Why did he do this?
   b. What effect do you think this probably had on them? Why?
3. Why was Garibaldi able, with only a small force, to defeat the much larger armies of the Kingdom of the Two Sicilies?
4. How does Garibaldi's success show the importance of the spirit of nationalism?

In this scene, the people of the Kingdom of the Two Sicilies are voting to join the Kingdom of Italy. Why do you think they wanted to join the new kingdom?

3. HOW DID ITALY COMPLETE ITS UNIFICATION?

The Kingdom of Italy was formed in 1861. It was a limited monarchy ruled by Victor Emmanuel, formerly the king of Sardinia. Its government was modeled on that of Great Britain, but, like the French system, it had many political parties.

The northern parts of Italy made economic progress after unification. The south, however, remained poor. Another problem was that the new kingdom did not include certain territories that were inhabited mainly by Italians. The Pope ruled over the city of Rome. The Austrians still occupied some regions in northern Italy. The map that follows shows how Italy gradually gained these "unredeemed" portions.

THE UNIFICATION OF ITALY

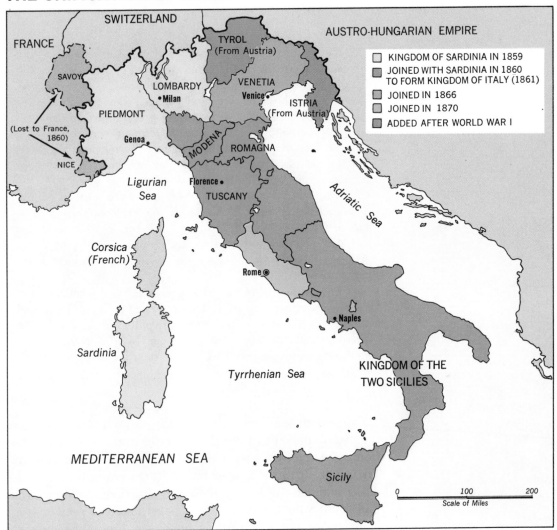

SWITZERLAND

FRANCE

AUSTRO-HUNGARIAN EMPIRE

TYROL
(From Austria)

SAVOY

LOMBARDY
•Milan

VENETIA

Venice•

ISTRIA
(From Austria)

PIEDMONT

(Lost to France,
1860)

Genoa•

MODENA

ROMAGNA

NICE

Ligurian
Sea

Florence •

TUSCANY

Adriatic Sea

Corsica
(French)

Rome ◉

•Naples

Sardinia

Tyrrhenian Sea

KINGDOM OF THE
TWO SICILIES

MEDITERRANEAN SEA

Sicily

	KINGDOM OF SARDINIA IN 1859
	JOINED WITH SARDINIA IN 1860 TO FORM KINGDOM OF ITALY (1861)
	JOINED IN 1866
	JOINED IN 1870
	ADDED AFTER WORLD WAR I

0   100   200
Scale of Miles

▶ INTERPRETING THE MAP

1. What territories were united in 1860 to form the Kingdom of
   Italy the following year?
2. Which territories joined the kingdom in 1866? In 1870?
   Which territories were lost in 1860?
3. Which territories were added after World War I?
4. The Kingdom of Italy fought three wars to gain these territories.
   Do you think unification was worth the costs? Why or why not?

4. *HOW WAS GERMAN NATIONALISM BORN?*

In the eighteenth century, Germany was even more disunited than Italy. Germany at that time consisted of some 200 to 300 different states, most of which were quite small. The two largest German states were Austria and Prussia. They were rivals for leadership of the smaller states. Prussia was a Protestant country, Austria a Catholic one. The rest of Germany was also divided between the two main Christian religions. The religious difference and the political rivalry between the two great powers kept Germany from being united.

In Germany, as in Italy, Napoleon stirred the spirit of nationalism and started the nation's unification. He conquered a large part of Germany, which he made into a single state under his rule. He defeated both Austria and Prussia. Finally, his harsh policies united the Germans against him and played an important part in his downfall.

The next selection is part of a speech made by Johann Fichte, a famous German professor. He appealed to his students, and through them to the German people, to unite. The city of Berlin, where he spoke, was then being occupied by French troops. Despite their presence, how was he able to arouse German nationalism?

Our oldest common ancestors, the Teutons [Germans], set themselves bravely against the powerful world-wide rule of the Romans. Didn't they want the advantages of Roman culture? Their descendants took over that culture as soon as they could do so without the loss of their own freedom. Freedom was their most valuable possession. They wanted to remain Germans and to continue settling their own affairs in their own way. Slavery was what they called all the benefits that the Romans offered them. Through those benefits they would become other than Germans. They would have to become half-Romans. It was perfectly clear, they thought, that every man would rather die. A true German could wish to live only to be and to remain a German, and to have his sons the same.

They have not all died. They have not seen slavery. They have left freedom to their children. We are the heirs of their land, their language, and their feelings. We owe to them that we are still Germans. Our problem today is to keep what is German. The higher love of the fatherland, for the entire people of the German nation, must remain supreme in every German state.

Adapted from G. C. Lee (ed.), *The World's Orators* (Vol. 5), p. 190.

▶ THINKING IT THROUGH

1. Because of special conditions, nationalism developed later in Germany than in most other European countries.
   a. Why was Germany *not* a geographic unit?
   b. What obstacles, other than lack of unity, slowed down the development of German nationalism?
2. "The unification of Germany was started by a Frenchman of Italian origin." Explain.
3. In the above speech, how does Fichte appeal to the nationalist feelings of his listeners?
4. Why was Fichte able to make nationalistic speeches like this one, even during the French occupation of Germany?

5. *WHY WAS BISMARCK APPOINTED THE FIRST MINISTER OF PRUSSIA?*

The Congress of Vienna gave little more regard to nationalism in Germany than in Italy. It left the German territories divided into thirty-eight states. They were joined in a weak union called the German Confederation. The revolutions of 1820, 1830, and 1848 did little to change this condition. Germany was finally united mainly through the efforts and skill of a Prussian nobleman, Prince OTTO VON BISMARCK.

In the next passage, Bismarck tells how William I, king of Prussia, called on him for help in 1862. The king wanted to strengthen the Prussian army. But the Prussian parliament refused to vote him the funds. What unusual methods does Bismarck admit he used to get the money the king wanted?

Otto von Bismarck, the first minister of Prussia, emphasizing a point while speaking before the Prussian legislature. Judging from this scene, what do you think was his attitude toward parliamentary government?

The situation became clear to me when His Majesty defined it in some such words as these, "I will not reign unless I can do so in a way that I can answer for to God, my conscience, and my subjects. But I cannot do that if I am to rule according to the will of the present majority in parliament. And I can

William I, the Prussian king who became emperor of Germany.

no longer find any ministers prepared to conduct my govern-ment without giving in to the parliamentary majority. I have, therefore, decided to lay down my crown. I have already worked out the announcement in which I will give up my throne." The king showed me the paper written in his own handwriting lying on the table.

I replied that His Majesty knew my readiness to become his first minister. The king asked whether I was prepared to insist on the reorganization of the army. He then asked whether I would do so in opposition to parliament. When I assured him I was willing, he finally declared, "Then it is my duty, with your help, to continue the battle. I shall not give up the throne."

In the beginning of October, I went to meet the king at Baden-Baden. My object in this interview was to set His Majesty at rest about a speech made by me in the budget commission on September 30. This speech had caused some excitement. I had shown plainly the direction in which I was going. Prussia—such was the point of my speech—could no longer carry alone the power that Germany required for its security. That must be equally distributed over all German peoples. [In other words, Prussia wanted to unite Germany under its leadership.] We would get no nearer our goal by speeches, associations, or decisions by majority. We would not be able to avoid a serious contest with Austria. This contest could only be settled by blood and iron [military power and war]. There is one way to guarantee our success. The deputies must place the greatest possible weight of blood and iron in the hands of the king of Prussia.

When I begged the king for permission to tell him what had happened, he interrupted. He said, "I can perfectly well see where all this will end. The people will cut off your head, and mine a little while afterwards." "Yes," I said, "then we shall be dead. But we must all die sooner or later. Can we perish more honorably? I, fighting for my king's cause, and Your Majesty sealing with your own blood your rights as king by the grace of God. Your Majesty is bound to fight. You cannot surrender. You must, even at the risk of bodily danger, go forth to meet any attempt to force your surrender." As I continued to speak in this way, the king grew more and more lively. He felt as though he had been touched in his military honor. He felt in the position of an officer who has orders to hold a certain position to the death. In a few minutes he was assured again, and even gained back his cheerfulness.

Adapted from Prince Otto von Bismarck, *Bismarck, The Man and the Statesman* (translated by A. J. Butler), p. 291.

▶ THINKING IT THROUGH

1. William I planned to give up the throne of Prussia.
   a. Why did he want to do so?
   b. How did Bismarck persuade him to stay in power?
2. Why did Bismarck become known as "the man of blood and iron"?
3. The king was afraid of a revolution in Prussia. How did Bismarck overcome his fear?
4. Bismarck defied Prussia's parliament and public opinion. Do you think he should have done so, even though many Germans disapproved? Explain.

6. HOW DID BISMARCK UNIFY GERMANY?

Bismarck very carefully planned the wars to unify Germany. First he involved Prussia in a quick war in 1864 with the small country of Denmark. He objected to the way Denmark treated the Germans living in the two Danish provinces of Schleswig and Holstein. (See the map on page 91.) His victory caused the rest of Germany to look to Prussia as the defender of the Germans.

After defeating Denmark, Prussia took over the two provinces. This led Austria to declare war on Prussia, just as Bismarck had expected. The Austro-Prussian War (1866) lasted only seven weeks. Bismarck's powerful new army easily crushed the Austrians. This victory made Prussia the leader of Germany. All the Protestant states now joined Prussia in a close union called the North German Confederation.

Bismarck's last step was to bring the Catholic German states into the union. He knew that a war with France, Germany's old enemy, would do this. The following passage is from Bismarck's memoirs. Notice the way in which he managed to get France to declare war on Germany.

On July 2, 1870, the Spanish government decided to ask Leopold, prince of Hohenzollern [the Prussian royal family], to take the throne of Spain. It was hard to find in the law of nations an excuse for France to interfere with the freedom of Spain to choose its own king. But the French demanded that Leopold refuse the throne.

Our foreign office answered that our ministry knew nothing about the matter. The question of Prince Leopold's acceptance was treated by His Majesty simply as a family matter. The insulting nature of the French demand was increased by threats in the French newspapers, discussions in their parliament, and a statement by their ministry. It declared, "The crowning of Prince Leopold will not come to pass, of that we are quite certain. Should it prove otherwise, we shall know how to fulfill our duty without shrinking and without weakness."

This was an official threat, with the hand on the sword hilt. In my feeling, it made any agreement on our part a violation of our sense of national honor. A week later, the prince gave up his candidacy in order to prevent the war with which France threatened us. My first idea was to retire from my position. I saw in this action a humiliation of Prussia, for which I did not desire to be responsible. I was very much depressed. I saw no means of repairing the injury to our national position from this timid policy.

Having decided to resign, I invited [Count Albrecht von] Roon [Prussia's War Minister] and [Count Helmuth von] Moltke [the commander of the army] to dine with me. I told them my plans and reasons. During our conversation, a telegram arrived from the king. I read it to them. The French now demanded that the king promise *never* to allow a Hohenzollern to accept the Spanish throne. I read it out to my guests. They were so downcast that they turned away from food and drink.

I looked over the telegram several times. Then I asked Moltke how much time he would need to meet this sudden risk of war. He said a rapid outbreak was more favorable to us than delay. In the presence of my two guests, I reduced the telegram by striking out some words, but without adding or changing anything. I read the shortened version to my two guests. Moltke then remarked, "Now it has a different ring. It sounded before like part of a discussion. Now it is like the answer to a challenge."

I went on to explain. "If I give this text to the newspapers immediately, it will be known in Paris before midnight. It will have the effect of a red rag upon the Gallic [French] bull. Fight

A Prussian battery firing on Paris during the Franco-Prussian War. The Prussians boasted of having the strongest, most modern army on the continent. How does this scene support their claim?

we must, if we do not want to act like a defeated nation without a battle. Success, however, depends on the impression which the start of the war makes. It is important that we should be the party attacked."

This explanation brought about in the two generals a change to a more joyful mood. The liveliness of it surprised me. They suddenly recovered their pleasure in eating and drinking. Roon said, "Our God of old still lives and will not let us perish in disgrace." Moltke struck his hand upon his breast and said, "If I may but live to lead our armies in such a war, then the devil may come directly afterwards to take away my old body."

Adapted from Prince Otto von Bismarck, *Bismarck, The Man and the Statesman* (translated by A. J. Butler), p. 100.

▶ **THINKING IT THROUGH**

1. Bismarck and his guests underwent a sudden change of mood.
   a. Why were they so depressed at first?
   b. Why did they become happy later?
   c. Should the thought of war have made them happy? Why or why not?
2. Bismarck deliberately changed the king's telegram.
   a. Do you approve of this action? Why or why not?
   b. Why did Bismarck say, "It will have the effect of a red flag on the Gallic bull"?
3. Bismarck boasted about this incident in his memoirs, which he wrote many years later. Should he have been proud of what he did? Why or why not?

Bismarck (left) and Napoleon III meeting to discuss peace terms after the Prussian forces have defeated the French. What do you suppose each of these men is thinking?

7. *WHAT TERRITORIES FORMED THE NEW GERMAN EMPIRE?*

As Bismarck had expected, the southern German states joined Prussia immediately after France declared war. The Germans quickly defeated the French, taking Napoleon III prisoner. The victors treated France harshly. They took the two border provinces of Alsace and Lorraine. They also collected 5 billion francs (about $1 billion) as payment for the costs of the war. The new GERMAN EMPIRE—a close union of all the German states except Austria—was proclaimed in the Palace of Versailles. The map that follows shows the steps by which German unification was achieved. Study the map; then answer the questions about it.

THE UNIFICATION OF GERMANY

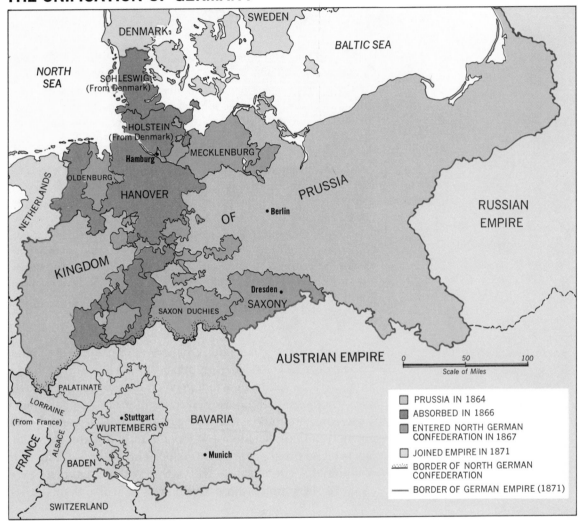

▶ **INTERPRETING THE MAP**

1. Which territories did Prussia take from Denmark in 1866?
2. Name three or four of the territories that made up the North German Confederation in 1867. Which do you think was the most important of these territories? Explain your choice.
3. What territories did Prussia take from France (in 1871)?
4. What important countries formed the borders of the German Empire that was created in 1871?

8. WHY DID GERMANY BECOME A GREAT POWER?

Bismarck was CHANCELLOR (prime minister) of the new German Empire, a position he held for almost twenty years. It was a time of great progress for the new nation. Germany surpassed Great Britain in industrial production and became a great trading nation. It was also known throughout the world for its schools and scientists.

Bismarck's government encouraged this progress by giving generous aid to industry, commerce, agriculture, and education. In addition to these achievements, Germany provided its workers with the most complete program of old age and sickness benefits to date.

Despite such advantages, however, the German people did not have much political power. You may wonder why an undemocratic government adopted such liberal policies. The next passage is an interview in which Bismarck explains his reasons for promoting these policies.

I went to the chancellor's palace at the appointed time. Prince Bismarck looked well and hearty. He said, "A beginning must be made in winning over the laboring classes. A man who has a pension assured to him for his old age is much more contented and easier to manage than the man who has no such outlook. Compare a servant in a private house and one attached to a government office. The latter looks forward to a pension. Therefore, he will put up with a great deal more, and will show much more willingness to work, than the former."

He paused for a moment, then continued, "Large sums of money would be required for carrying out such schemes—at least 100 million marks [$25 million], or more probably, 200 million marks [$50 million]. But I would not be frightened by even 300 millions [$75 million]. Means must be provided to enable the state to act generously towards the poor. The contentment of all those who have no possessions is worth buying even at a very high figure. They must also learn that the state benefits them too—that it not only demands, but also gives.

Adapted from Moritz Busch, *Bismarck* (Vol. II).

William I is proclaimed German emperor while Bismarck and the German military leaders look on. The ceremony is taking place in the French palace of Versailles. How do you think the French felt about the coronation being held in their historic palace?

▶ THINKING IT THROUGH

1. In this passage, Bismarck explains why he established government insurance for sickness and old age.
   a. What reasons does he give?
   b. Do you agree with his reasons? Why or why not?
2. Bismarck's military successes weakened democracy in Germany.
   a. Why do you think this was so?
   b. How do you think his later reforms affected the development of German democracy?
3. Why do many Germans consider Bismarck one of their great leaders? Do you agree with their attitude? Why or why not?

9. HOW DID NATIONALISM BREAK UP THREE EMPIRES?

In Italy and Germany, nationalism served as a force for unity. In each of these areas, it urged people living in several separate states to form a united nation. Nationalism does not only promote unity, however. It can also cause larger states to splinter. It has led to the breakup of three large empires inhabited by people of different nationalities.

The maps on page 94 show how nationalism affected the Austrian, Ottoman, and Russian Empires. The first map shows Europe and the Near East after the Congress of Vienna. The second map shows the effects of nationalism a century later, after World War I. Notice how many subject nationalities had gained their independence from foreign rule.

EUROPE IN 1815

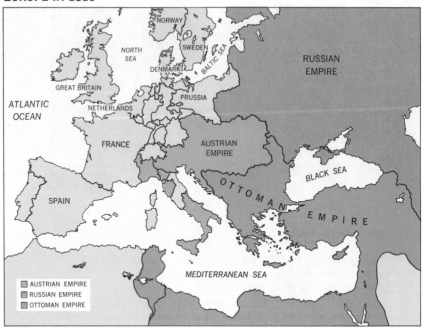

EUROPE IN 1919

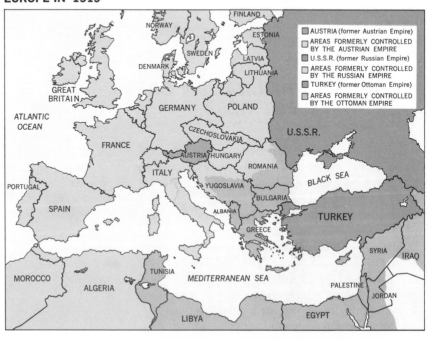

▶ INTERPRETING THE MAPS

1. After World War I, what large country occupied most of the territory that formerly constituted the Russian Empire? Name two or three smaller countries that also now existed.
2. What empire did Turkey emerge from?
3. What happened to the Austrian Empire after World War I?
4. From which empires was each of the following states formed:
    a. Romania.
    b. Yugoslavia.
    c. Poland.
5. Judging from these maps, how do you think nationalism affected the former Austrian, Ottoman, and Russian Empires?

10. IS NATIONALISM STILL A STRONG FORCE TODAY?

Nationalism is still very powerful in the world today. During the early twentieth century, Asia and Africa felt its impact. Most European possessions on both continents gained independence after World War II. Still nationalism continues to cause unrest, conflicts, and civil wars, as the following news headlines show.

ARABS KILL 11 ISRAELI ATHLETES AT OLYMPIC GAMES

BOMBINGS AND SHOOTINGS CONTINUE IN NORTHERN IRELAND
Civil war between Catholics and Protestants may result

BIAFRA SURRENDERS
Ibos give up war for independence from Nigeria

ERITREANS DEMAND LIBERATION FROM ETHIOPIA
Local fighting reported

SIKHS DEMAND INDEPENDENT STATE IN INDIA

PATHANS TRY TO BREAK AWAY FROM PAKISTAN

▶ **THINKING IT THROUGH**

1. These headlines reveal some of the effects of modern nationalism.
   a. Which effects seem to be stronger today—those that tend to unify nations or those that tend to break them up? Support your answer.
   b. Nationalism has been called "the most explosive force in the modern world." Do you agree with this observation? Why or why not?

2. Suppose that each nationality in the United States were to demand independence.
   a. What would happen to this country?
   b. Is there any possibility that this might happen? Why or why not?

3. The number of nations that are members of the United Nations has risen from 50 in 1945 to about 150 today.
   a. What does this increase show about the effects of nationalism in recent years?
   b. Some of the new member nations of the United Nations are so small in area and population that they are sometimes referred to as "mini-states." Is it a good idea for such small places to become independent nations? Why or why not?

4. The noted American folk singer Joan Baez has said, "I have contempt for all flags. A flag is a symbol of a piece of territory that is considered to be more important than the men who live in it. We have to rid ourselves of the concept of nations." Do you agree with this observation? Why or why not?

Reviewing Chapter 5

SUMMING UP

1. Why is it that Mazzini was called "the soul of Italian unification," Cavour its "brain," and Garibaldi its "sword"?
2. Did Bismarck deserve all three titles of soul, brain, and sword in Germany? Why or why not?
3. Explain how nationalism has served each of the following purposes:
   a. It has tended to unify nations.

b. It has helped to break up nations.
c. It has led to conflicts between different groups within nations.
4. Should nationalism be replaced by *internationalism*? (This is the belief that all people, regardless of their nationality, should work together to promote the common interests of all mankind.) Explain.

FOR FURTHER INQUIRY

1. Patriotism is love of fatherland—that is, devotion to one's country. Nationalism has been defined as extreme patriotism.
   a. Should people be patriotic?
   b. Should they be nationalistic?
   Explain each answer.
2. Italy and Germany became united nations much later than the rest of Europe.
   a. Why did this happen?
   b. As a result, would you expect the Italians and Germans to be more or less nationalistic than other Europeans? Explain.
3. Did the spirit of nationalism strengthen or weaken democracy in Italy? In Germany? Support each answer.
4. "The German chancellor is responsible only to the emperor, and the emperor is responsible only to God."

a. Why did Bismarck write this provision into the constitution of the new German Empire?
b. The German Empire had a parliament, yet its government has been called a "veiled absolutism." Was this an accurate description? Why or why not?
c. Why did the German people accept and support this government for many years?
5. "Nationalism has been a force for both unity and disunity in the modern world."
   a. Explain this statement.
   b. Which effect of nationalism do you think is stronger today. Why?
   c. What can the government of a state containing several nationalities do to unify the various peoples within its borders?

ROLE-PLAYING: DEBATE

Resolved: Nationalism Is Outdated Today

Be prepared to take the role of a speaker for either side of a debate on nationalism. The side maintaining that nationalism is out-of-date should stress the evils of nationalism. It should also speak of the advantages of international cooperation. The side favoring nationalism should explain the strengths and benefits of patriotism. The class should ask questions and decide whether nationalism is still meaningful.

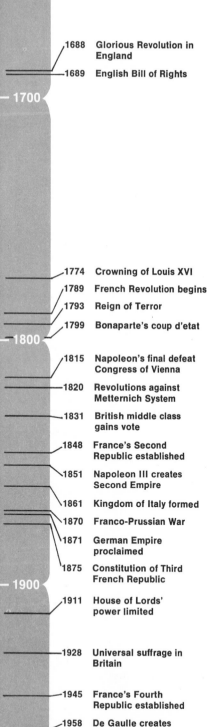

1649   Execution of Charles I

1688   Glorious Revolution in England

1689   English Bill of Rights

— 1700

1774   Crowning of Louis XVI

1789   French Revolution begins

1793   Reign of Terror

1799   Bonaparte's coup d'etat

—1800

1815   Napoleon's final defeat Congress of Vienna

1820   Revolutions against Metternich System

1831   British middle class gains vote

1848   France's Second Republic established

1851   Napoleon III creates Second Empire

1861   Kingdom of Italy formed

1870   Franco-Prussian War

1871   German Empire proclaimed

1875   Constitution of Third French Republic

— 1900

1911   House of Lords' power limited

1928   Universal suffrage in Britain

1945   France's Fourth Republic established

1958   De Gaulle creates Fifth Republic

ENRICHING YOUR UNDERSTANDING

▶ REACHING OUT

1. The terms conservative, liberal, radical, and reactionary have been used to describe political beliefs.
   a. Define each of these terms.
   b. Which term best describes your thinking? Explain your answer.
2. Which viewpoint was strongest in Great Britain, France, Italy, and Germany during the period discussed in this chapter? Explain briefly in each case.
3. "The basic viewpoint of an individual or a political party tends to remain the same for many years. But its specific program keeps changing."
   a. Why is this so?
   b. Why is yesterday's radical often today's liberal or conservative?

▶ INTERPRETING THE TIME LINE

The development of democracy and nationalism in Western civilization has been the main theme of this book. Both of these movements helped to create new forms of government in the West. The time line on this page shows how some of these new forms came into being. Examine it carefully, then answer the questions that follow.

1. What were some of the important steps in the development of British democracy?
2. What different types of government are shown on this time line for France? What does this suggest about the nature of the French system? Explain.
3. Which events show the influence of nationalism? Explain.
4. How old is the Italian nation? The German nation? Why are these countries considered new nations?

98

Alderman, Clifford L. *Liberty, Equality, Fraternity* (Messner, 1965). The colorful story of the French Revolution.

Almedingen, E. M. *The Retreat from Moscow* (Warne, 1968). A moving account of one of the greatest military disasters in history.

Apsler, Alfred. *Iron Chancellor* (Messner, 1968). A biography of Otto von Bismarck, the statesman who unified Germany.

Baker, Nina B. *Garibaldi* (Vanguard, 1944). A dramatic true account of "the sword of Italian unification."

Eimerl, Sarel. *Revolution! France, 1789–1794* (Little, Brown, 1967). An outstanding account of the events that changed France.

Fisher, John. *Six Summers in Paris* (Harper & Row, 1967). A historical fiction about the leaders and events of the Revolution described by a supposed eyewitness.

Hatch, Alden. *The De Gaulle Nobody Knows* (Hawthorn, 1960). A biography of the general who founded France's Fifth Republic.

Hibbert, Christopher. *Garibaldi and His Enemies* (Little, Brown, 1966). A very full and dramatic account of the Italian hero.

Holt, Victoria. *The Queen's Confession* (Doubleday, 1968). The tragic story of Queen Marie Antoinette, told in the first person.

Horizon Magazine editors and David L. Dowd. *The French Revolution* (American Heritage, 1965). A well-written and well-illustrated account.

Komroff, Manuel. *Napoleon* (Messner, 1954). An outstanding simple biography of the brilliant French military leader and emperor.

Komroff, M. and O. Komroff. *Marie Antoinette* (Messner). The story of the unfortunate French queen who was beheaded during the Revolution.

Loomis, Stanley. *Paris in the Terror.* (Lippincott, 1964). An interesting account, based on eyewitness descriptions of the Reign of Terror.

Maurois, Andre. *Napoleon: A Biography with Pictures* (Viking, 1964). One of the leading biographies of Napoleon.

Noble, Iris. *Emmeline and Her Daughters* (Messner, 1971). Tells why Emmeline Pankhurst and her three daughters became militant suffragettes, and what they accomplished by using violence.

ACKNOWLEDGMENTS

PRINTED MATERIALS

We are grateful to the following authors, companies, and agencies for their permission to use copyrighted material:

BRITISH INFORMATION SERVICES
The United Kingdom Constitution: Some Selected Quotations. Adapted by permission.

GINN AND COMPANY, A XEROX COMPANY
Cheyney, E. P., *Readings in European History.* Adapted by permission.
Robinson, James Harvey (ed.), *Readings in European History.* Adapted by permission.

HAWTHORN BOOKS, INC. PUBLISHERS
Adapted from *The de Gaulle Nobody Knows* by Alden Hatch. Copyright © 1960 by Alden Hatch. By permission of Hawthorn Books, Inc.

INTERNATIONAL PUBLISHERS COMPANY, INC.
Marx, Karl. *The Class Struggles in France,* 1935. Reprinted by permission.

J. B. LIPPINCOTT COMPANY
Adapted from the book *Paris in the Terror: June 1793–July 1794,* by Stanley Loomis. Copyright © 1964 by Stanley Loomis. Reprinted by permission of J. B. Lippincott Company.

LIVERIGHT PUBLISHING CORPORATION
Ludwig, Emil. *Napoleon.* Adapted by permission.

LOS ANGELES TIMES
June 21, 1970. Copyright (1970), *Los Angeles Times.* Reprinted by permission.

THE MACMILLAN COMPANY
Stewart, John Hall, *A Documentary Survey of the French Revolution* (© Copyright, The Macmillan Company 1951).

NEWSWEEK
Copyright Newsweek, Inc. 1969, reprinted by permission.

RAND MCNALLY AND COMPANY
Adapted from George L. Mosse et al (eds.), *Europe in Review,* Rev., © 1957, 1964 by Rand McNally and Company, Chicago. Used by permission.

RUTGERS UNIVERSITY PRESS
Snyder, Louis L. (trans.), *Documents of German History*. Adapted by permission.

TIME, THE WEEKLY NEWSMAGAZINE
Reprinted by permission from *Time, The Weekly Newsmagazine;* Copyright Time Inc. November 10, 1967.

The authors wish to state that every effort has been made to locate the following authors or their heirs to obtain permission to reprint or adapt selections from their works: Prince Otto von Bismarck, *Bismarck, The Man and the Statesman* (translated by A. J. Butler), and Emmeline Pankhurst, *My Own Story*. If any of these authors or their heirs are located subsequent to publication, they are hereby entitled to due compensation.

PHOTOGRAPHS

The photographs included in this text, on the pages indicated below, appear courtesy of the following:

Austrian Information Service (By courtesy of the Austrian Information Service, New York), 55

The Bettmann Archive, 1, 3, 4, 5, 11, 14, 23, 29, 30, 35, 37, 38, 46, 61, 62, 64, 66, 67, 78, 80, 81, 85, 89, 90

British Museum, 8

Coronet Instructional Media, 9, 19, 24 (top), 44, 71

European Art Color Slides/Peter Adelberg, Inc., 24 (bottom), 43, 49, 51, 53

FPG/Photoworld, 17

French Embassy Press and Information Division, 31, 33, 34, 72, 93

New York Public Library, 6, 54, 77, 82

Springer/Bettmann Film Archive, 10

U.S. Signal Corps Photo, 86

INDEX

Directory. *See* French Revolution of 1789.

Rights, 8-9; democracy in, 3-4; Glorious Revolution of 1688, 8-9, 10; limited monarchy, 10-11, 14, Magna Carta, 3-4; Parliament, 4-5, 6-7, 20; prime minister, 12-13; Reform Bill, 14-15; republic, 8; universal suffrage, 15-16; wars with France, 34; women's rights, 16-17. *See also* Europe; Republic.

Greece, 2

Guillotine, the, 38

S

Sardinia, 80, 82
Second Estate, the. *See* France.
Second Republic (French). *See* France.
Sicily, 70, 80
Socialism, 63
Spain, 34, 51, 56, 88, 89. *See also* Europe.
Suffragettes, 16-17
Stael, Madame Germaine de, 45-46
St. Helena, 52

T

Taille, 25, 26, 27. *See also* Taxes.
Taxes, in France, 23; in Great Britain, 5, 9, 15. *See also Taille;* Tithe.
Teutons, 84
Third Estate. *See* France.
Third Republic (French). *See* France.
Thousand Red Shirts, the, 80-81
Three Estates, the. *See* France.
Tithe, 32. *See also* Taxes.
Tocqueville, Alexis de, 61-62
Tories, 19. *See also* Conservatives.
Turkish Empire, 1. *See also* Ottoman Empire.

Two-party system, in Great Britain, 12

U

Universal suffrage, in Great Britain, 15; *graph,* 16

V

Versailles, 30, 31, 90
Vichy government, 70
Victor Emmanuel (king of Sardinia and of Italy), 82
Vienna, Austria, 54. *See also* Congress of Vienna.

W

Waterloo, 52
Whigs, 14. *See also* Liberals.
William I (king of Prussia and emperor of Germany), 85-87, 88-90. *See also* Germany.
William of Orange (king of England), 8
Wilson, Harold, 12
Worker class, 1, 38,; uprising in France, 61-62, 63-64
World War I, 69, 93
World War II, 70, 95